W9-BKJ-829

NO TIME LIKE THE PRESENT

NO TIME LIKE THE PRESENT

*Finding Freedom, Love, and Joy
Right Where You Are*

JACK KORNFIELD

ATRIA BOOKS

New York • London • Toronto • Sydney • New Delhi

ATRIA
BOOKS

An Imprint of Simon & Schuster, Inc.
1230 Avenue of the Americas
New York, NY 10020

First Atria Books hardcover edition May 2017

ATRIA BOOKS and colophon are trademarks of Simon & Schuster, Inc.

For information about special discounts for bulk purchases, please contact Simon & Schuster Special Sales at 1-866-506-1949 or business@simonandschuster.com.

The Simon & Schuster Speakers Bureau can bring authors to your live event. For more information or to book an event, contact the Simon & Schuster Speakers Bureau at 1-866-248-3049 or visit our website at www.simonspeakers.com.

Interior design by Dana Sloan

Manufactured in the United States of America

10 9 8 7 6 5 4 3 2

Library of Congress Cataloging-in-Publication Data

Names: Kornfield, Jack, 1945- author.
Title: No time like the present : finding freedom, love, and joy right where you are / By Jack Kornfield.
Description: New York, NY : Atria Books, [2017] | Includes index. | Description based on print version record and CIP data provided by publisher; resource not viewed.
Identifiers: LCCN 2016052941 (print) | LCCN 2017012274 (ebook) | ISBN 9781451693713 (eBook) | ISBN 9781451693690 (hardcover) | ISBN 9781451693706 (pbk.)
Subjects: LCSH: Spiritual life.
Classification: LCC BL624 (ebook) | LCC BL624 .K674 2017 (print) | DDC 204/.4—dc23
LC record available at https://lccn.loc.gov/2016052941

ISBN 978-1-4516-9369-0
ISBN 978-1-4516-9371-3 (ebook)

To my twin brother,
Irv

An adventurer, a lover of life,
an unbridled spirit

A bird doesn't sing because it has an answer, it sings because it has a song.

—JOAN WALSH ANGLUND

Contents

Contents

Invitation to Freedom

Dear friends, after more than forty years teaching mindfulness and compassion to thousands on the spiritual path, the most important message I can offer is this: *You don't have to wait to be free. You don't need to postpone being happy.*

All too often the beautiful spiritual practices of mindfulness and compassion become entwined with a vision of self-discipline and duty. We see them as taking us through a long road of obstacles that leads eventually to distant benefits. Yes, there is hard work of the heart, and there are demanding cycles in our lives. Yet wherever you are on your journey, there is another wonderful truth called "Living the Fruit" or "Starting with the Result." The fruits of well-being and the experience of joy, freedom, and love are available now, whatever your circumstance!

When Nelson Mandela walked out of Robben Island prison after twenty-seven years of incarceration, he did so with such dignity, magnanimity, and forgiveness that his spirit transformed South Africa and inspired the world. Like Mandela, you can be free and dignified wherever you find yourself. However difficult your circumstances, however uncertain the times, remember, freedom is not reserved for exceptional people. No one can imprison your spirit.

When your boss calls and you feel fear or anxiety, when someone in your family is in conflict or duress, when you feel overwhelmed by the growing problems of the world, you have choices. You can be bound and constricted, or you can use this difficulty to open and discover how to respond wisely in this unfolding journey. Sometimes life gives us ease, sometimes it is challenging, and sometimes profoundly painful. Sometimes the whole society around you is in upheaval. Whatever your circumstances, you can take a breath, soften your gaze, and remember that courage and freedom are within, waiting for you to awaken, and to offer to others. Even under the direst conditions, freedom of spirit is available. Freedom of spirit is mysterious, magnificent, and simple. We are free and able to love in this life—no matter what.

Deep down we know this is true. We know it whenever we feel a part of something greater—listening to music, making love, walking in the mountains or swimming in the sea, sitting with the mystery of a dying loved one as her spirit leaves her body silently as a falling star, or witnessing the miraculous birth of a child. At times like these, a joyful openness swells through our body, and our heart is surrounded by peace.

Freedom starts where we are. Sara, a single mom with two

kids, found out that her eight-year-old daughter, Alicia, had leukemia. Sara was terrified, anxious, grieving the loss of her child's health, scared that she would lose her. For the first year, Alicia went through long rounds of chemotherapy, hospital stays, and doctors. A fearful sadness filled the house, and anxiety colored Sara's days. Then, one afternoon when they were out on a walk, Alicia said, "Mama, I don't know how long I'm going to live, but I want them to be happy days."

Her words were a splash of cold water on her mother's face. Sara realized that she had to step out of the fearful melodrama to meet her daughter's freedom of mind with her own, to return to a trusting spirit. Sara grabbed her daughter and did a little waltz, holding her tight. Her fear dissipated. And in time, Alicia healed. She is now twenty-two and just graduated from college.

But even if she hadn't healed, what kind of days would you have had her choose? You can't do much with your life if you're miserable. You might as well be happy.

When I was eight years old, on an especially bitter, windy winter day, my brothers and I dressed in jackets, scarves, and gloves and went out to play in the snow. I was skinny as a rail and shivering with cold. My twin brother, Irv, stronger, wilder, and more robust, looked at me, contracted and fearful, and laughed. Then he began to remove layers of clothing, first the gloves, his coat, then a sweater, his shirt, undershirt, all the while laughing. He danced and paraded around half-naked in the snow, the icy wind whipping around us. We were all wide-eyed, laughing hysterically.

In that moment, my brother taught me about choosing freedom, manifesting a spirit that to this day I still remember. Whether we're in a wildly blowing snowstorm or feeling the cold wind of loss, blame, or of our collective insecurity, we want to be free. We want to be released from fear and worry, not confined by judgments. We can. We can learn to trust, love, express ourselves, and be happy.

As we discover trust and freedom in ourselves, we will then find our way to share them with the world. Barbara Wiedner, who founded Grandmothers for Peace, explains, "I began to question the kind of a world I am leaving for my grandchildren. So, I got a sign, 'A Grandmother for Peace,' and stood on a street corner. Then I joined others kneeling as a human barrier at a munitions factory. I was taken to prison, strip-searched, and thrown into a cell. Something happened to me. I realized they couldn't do anything more. I was free!" Now Barbara and her organization, Grandmothers for Peace, works in dozens of countries around the world.

This same freedom is here for you as well. Each chapter of this book is an invitation to experience a particular dimension of freedom—we begin personally, with freedom of spirit, freedom to start over, freedom beyond fear, freedom to be yourself, and then discover freedom to love, freedom to stand up for what matters, freedom to be happy. There are stories, reflections, teachings, and practices that illuminate how we get stuck and how we can free ourselves. This isn't a book that you read just to make yourself feel better for a little while and then put on your shelf. Finding freedom is an active process that engages your intellect, your heart, and your whole spirit. The means and the goal are one: be yourself, dream, trust, have courage, and act.

You can choose your spirit. Freedom, Love, and Joy are yours, in your very life, your exact circumstance. They are your birthright.

Jack Kornfield
Spirit Rock Meditation Center
Spring 2017

Part One

Freedom of Spirit

What do you plan to do with this one
wild and precious life?

—MARY OLIVER

Chapter 1

Vastness Is Our Home

*Sometimes I go about pitying myself, when all the while
I am being carried by great winds across the sky.*

—OJIBWA SAYING

We are being carried on a luminous star, sharing in the dance of life with seven billion beings like us. Vastness is our home. When we recognize the spaciousness that is our universe, around us and within us, the door of freedom opens. Worries and conflicts fall into perspective, emotions are held with ease, and we act amid troubles of the world with peace and dignity.

The Dance of Life

Whitney was caught in midlife troubles. Her mother was scheduled for hip surgery, and her father was suffering from early-stage

Alzheimer's. She wanted her parents to continue living in their home in Illinois, but their disabilities made independent living challenging. Whitney's brother in St. Louis was not involved and wanted his sister to "take care of it." So, Whitney took a month's leave from work and went to her parents' home to help. When she arrived, the house was in shambles. Her mom needed time to heal from the surgery, and her father was unable to care for himself. They could not afford round-the-clock care, and it was clear they would have to move.

Whitney took a walk up a hillside she'd known since childhood. She didn't want to lose the family home; she wanted her parents to stay there until the end—and she didn't want to lose her parents. She wept as she walked, but when she reached the top of the hill, she sat quietly, calmed herself, and looked across the vast midwestern fields stretching to the horizon. The sky was filled with cumulus clouds bringing shade to the many small houses clustered at the edge of town and beyond.

Facing this unbounded vastness, she suddenly felt less alone. She could sense how everything has its rhythm—arriving and departing, flourishing and struggling, coming into being and fading away. *How many people,* she wondered, *are in the same predicament we are in right now?* As she breathed with more ease, her mind opened further. *I am not the only person with aging parents. It is part of the human journey.* And as the space within her opened, she felt more trust.

We can all see this way. We can gain a broader perspective. With a spacious heart, we can remember the bigger picture. Even when illness strikes, a parent is dying, or any other form of loss is upon us, we can recognize that it's a part of life's seasons.

What would it feel like to love the whole kit and caboodle—to make our love bigger than our sorrows? Among the multitudes of humans, many are experiencing loss and change. Many need renewal. And still the world keeps turning, farmers growing food, markets trading, musicians playing. We live in the midst of a great and ever-changing paradox.

Breathe. Relax. Live each day one at a time.

The One Who Knows

As your spacious heart opens, you can rediscover the vast perspective you'd almost forgotten. The spacious heart reveals the spacious mind. This is the mind that, after you've stubbed your toe, hopped around, and howled, finally laughs. The mind that, when you are upset with your partner, goes to sleep, wakes up, and sees that what was such a big deal has fallen into perspective.

Your spacious mind is the natural awareness that knows and accommodates everything. My meditation teacher in the forests of Thailand, Ajahn Chah, called it "the One Who Knows." He said this is the original nature of mind, the silent witness, spacious consciousness. His instructions were simple: become witness to it all, the person with perspective, the One Who Knows.

Pay attention to the movie showing in your life right now. Notice the plot. It might be an adventure, a tragedy, a romance, a soap opera, or a battle. "All the world's a stage," wrote Shakespeare. Sometimes you get caught in the plot. But remember, you are also the audience. Take a breath. Look around. Become witness to it all, the spacious awareness, the One Who Knows.

I sat at the bedside of a woman with pancreatic cancer near the end of her days. She was only thirty-one years old. We looked in each other's eyes, and the layers just peeled away. Her skinny body, her gender, her poetic accomplishments, her family and friends. I was graced to be a witness to her spirit. "How's it going?" I asked, with great gentleness. "It looks like this incarnation is going to be over soon. It's okay. It's natural to die, you know." And what peered back through her deep, knowing eyes were vastness, tenderness, and a timeless freedom.

Rest in spacious awareness and feel the presence of love. The One Who Knows becomes the loving witness of all things. You become loving awareness itself. The freedom of loving awareness is available; it just takes practice for you to remember it and to trust that it is always here. When you feel lost, stuck in a tiny part of the big picture, contracted, or caught up, take a breath and visualize yourself stepping back. With a spacious mind, you can witness even these contracted states and hold them in loving awareness.

Relax. With loving awareness, you can notice your feelings, your thoughts, your circumstances. Just now. Even as you read this book, witness the one reading and smile at him or her with loving awareness. Begin each morning with loving awareness. Tune in to the space around you, the space outside, the huge landscape that spreads across the continent. Feel the vastness of the sky and of the space that holds the moon and planets and galaxies.

Let your mind and heart *become* that space. Breathe into your heart. Observe the clouds floating in the endless sky and become the sky. The clouds are not just outside; they are in you as well. Feel the landscape, the trees, the mountains, and buildings all arising in your own heart. Let yourself open, merge into space with love. Relax and rest in the immensity that surrounds you, the immensity that is you. Notice how vast loving awareness can be.

As the One Who Knows, witness it all, let loving awareness make room for everything: boredom *and* excitement, fear *and* trust, pleasure *and* pain, birth *and* death.

Sacred Stillness

When you walk into a shaded grove of giant redwoods or into a great cathedral, a sacred stillness descends. As spaciousness opens within you, you can experience a profound silence in your very being. You may feel nervous at first, and at the same time, you've longed for this. This is the vast silence that surrounds life. Trust it and rest in the stillness. Feel your heart open and become more fully alive. Everything that arises from this silence is only a cloud in the vast sky, a wave on the ocean. Rest in the depths of silence.

Vastness is the nature of consciousness. If you gaze at it directly, you'll discover that the mind is transparent, spacious, that it has no boundaries, that your heart is as wide as the world. As you open to this vastness, you can allow the waves of life to arise and pass. In silence, you'll see the mystery giving birth to life, to thoughts and feelings and sense perceptions. The waves of the world rise and fall, expand and contract, the heart beats, cerebral spinal fluid pulses, there are ever-changing rhythms in the phases of the moon, the changing of seasons, the cycles of a woman's body, the turning galaxies, and the stock market, too.

Begin to notice that there are pauses between the waves, gaps between breaths and between thoughts. At first these seem fleeting, but gradually you'll be able to rest in these pauses. As the waves rise and fall, you *become* silent loving awareness itself. This silence is not withdrawal, indifference, or punishment. It is not the absence of thoughts. It is spacious and refreshing, a tender stillness from which you can learn, listen, and look deeply.

Loving Awareness

Notice how loving awareness fills time and space. This is the mystery witnessing itself. In loving awareness, the river of thoughts and images flows without judgment. With loving awareness, you experience the stream of feelings without being afraid, falling under their spell, or grasping too tightly. Delight and anxiety, anger, tenderness, and longing, even grief and tears are all welcome. And loving awareness encourages the full measure of joy, inviting well-being to grow.

As you rest in loving awareness, trust grows. You trust the universe to run itself, and you trust your awareness to hold it all. I remember when I first learned to swim in the university pool.

I was a shivering, skinny seven-year-old. I flailed and bobbed around. And then, one moment, being held by the instructor as I lay on my back, he removed his hand and I realized I could float. It was magic. I learned to swim. In the same way, you can learn to trust loving awareness. It will always hold you.

As an experiment, try *not* to be aware. Take thirty seconds right now and stop being aware of any sense impressions, thoughts, feelings, and so forth. Try hard. Even if you close your eyes and plug your ears, it doesn't work, does it? You can't stop it. Awareness is always here.

Like the fish that can't see the water, you cannot see awareness directly. But you can experience it and therefore trust it. Loving awareness is spacious, open, transparent, silent, vast, and responsive like a mirror. You can always return to it. It is timeless, awake, and appreciative. Loving awareness sees without possessing. It allows, honors, connects, and dances with life as it is. It appreciates but does not grasp experiences or things. Author Steven Wright elucidates, "I have the world's largest collection of seashells. I keep it on all the beaches of the world. Perhaps you've seen it."

Running from Hyenas

Benjamin, age sixty-four, lost more than half his retirement savings in the 2008 economic crisis. He knew that he and his wife were better off than others whose mortgages went underwater and were losing their homes, but he became almost sick with anxiety. He checked the stock market ten times a day. His dreams were filled with images of drowning, being chased by hyenas, losing his way. His family told him to stop obsessing, but he didn't know how. When he came to his first meditation class, it was nearly impossible for him to sit still. Anxiety generated feelings in his body that were hard to accept, and his mind was racing. Should he pull his remaining money out of the badly lowered stocks? Might he lose more by abandoning a questionable real estate venture?

At the second class he attended, I led a guided meditation on space, inviting vast open awareness to surround body and mind. Students listened to the Tibetan bells in the room and the distant traffic and voices outside, listening as though their minds were as big as the sky and all the sounds were clouds within it. This experience brought Benjamin a sense of relief, and he bought a meditation CD to take home. After that, when anxious thoughts woke him in the night, he had a way to work with them. With vast space as his mantra, the grip of his obsession began to loosen. Now he had some perspective. He knew he could safeguard what remained of his money and invest more conservatively. He also relaxed the need to imagine he could control the future. Freed from obsessive thoughts, he was able to be present with his family again.

Shifts like Benjamin's are possible for everyone. We all remember times we've felt spacious and calm. We listen better, see more clearly, exercise more perspective. With spacious awareness, our inner life becomes clearer, too. Difficult emotions get clarified, their energy freed. Depression reveals its message about hurt, anger, and unmet needs. Fearful stories, when seen clearly, are lovingly open to release. The freedom of a spacious mind and heart is always available. Turn toward it. Open to vastness whenever you can. Become the sky of loving awareness.

Rest in Love

Spaciousness, awareness, and love are intertwined. I heard Frank Ostaseski, a friend who cofounded the Zen Hospice in San Francisco, tell the story of a resident there in a great deal of pain, who asked if learning meditation could help. He had terminal stomach cancer. They began to meditate by turning a kind attention toward the physical sensations.

But as he tried to open to these sensations, it was too intense for him and he screamed, "I can't, it's too much. It hurts, it hurts, it hurts." Frank told him okay, let's try something else and put his own hand gently on the man's stomach and said how's that? He said, "Oh, that hurts too much." "Let's try this," Frank went on, and put his hands near the man's feet. He said, "Ah, that's a little better." Then Frank put his hands a foot or two away from the man's body. And he said, "That's lovely actually."

This was no special form of body work, no esoteric practice. Just an opening to more and more space. After a few minutes, from a more relaxed face, the fellow said softly, "Oh, rest in love, rest in love." After that, whenever he'd get in trouble with his pain, he would push his morphine pump and then just repeat to himself, "Rest in love, rest in love."

It's really simple. Whether it's physical or emotional pain, anything you give space to can be transformed. Whatever the situation, widen the space; remember vastness; allow ease and perspective. Spaciousness is the doorway to freedom. Your spacious heart is your true home.

PRACTICE
Opening to Spacious Awareness

Think of a time in your life when you felt the most expansive, open, and loving. It may have been walking in the mountains, looking at the night sky filled with stars, or after the birth of a child. Remember how spacious awareness feels in your body. How it feels in the heart. Let the mind quiet. Remember how silent it was, how present you could be.

Now close your eyes. Feel that same vastness here and now. Relax and become the space of loving awareness that can allow sunshine, storm clouds, lightning, praise and blame, gain and loss, expansion and contraction, the world endlessly giving birth to itself, all with your gracious and peaceful heart.

PRACTICE
Mind Like the Sky

Sit comfortably and at ease. Let your body be at rest and your breath natural. Close your eyes. Take several full breaths and let each breath release gently. Allow yourself to be still.

Now shift your awareness away from the breath. Listen to the play of sounds around you. Notice whether they are loud or soft, far or near. Just listen. Notice how all sounds arise and vanish, leaving no trace. Listen for a while in a relaxed, open way.

As you listen, let yourself sense or imagine that your mind is not limited to your head. Sense that your mind is expanding to be like the sky—open, clear, vast like space. There is no inside or outside. Let the awareness of your mind extend in every direction, like the sky.

Allow the sounds you hear to arise and pass away in the open sky of your mind. Relax in this huge openness and just listen. Let the sounds come and go, far and near, like clouds in the vast sky of your own awareness. The sounds play through the sky, appearing and disappearing without resistance.

Then, as you rest in this open awareness, notice how thoughts and images also arise and vanish. They are like clouds. Let the thoughts and images come and go without struggle or resistance. Pleasant and unpleasant thoughts, pictures, words, and feelings move unrestricted in the space of mind. Problems, possibilities, joys, and sorrows come and go in the vast open sky of mind.

After a time, let this spacious awareness notice the body. Become aware of how the body is not solid. The sensations of breath and body float and change in the same open sky of awareness. In awareness, the body can be felt as floating areas of hardness and softness, pressure and tingling, warm and cool sensations, all appearing in the space of the mind's awareness. Notice, too, how the breath breathes itself; it moves like a breeze.

Let all experience be like clouds. The breath moves as it

will. Sensations float and change. Allow all thoughts and images, feelings and sounds to come and go, floating in the clear open space of awareness.

Finally, pay attention to the awareness itself. Notice how the open space of awareness is naturally clear, transparent, timeless, without conflict, allowing all things to be but not limited by them. Remember the pure open sky of your own true nature. Return to it. Trust it. It is home.

Chapter 2

Free to Love

*What good is a clear mind if not wedded
to a tender heart?*

We all want to love and be loved. Love is the natural order, the main attraction, the mover of nations, the bees in spring, the tender touch, the first and the last word. It is like gravity, a mysterious force that ties all things together, the heart's memory of being in the womb and the oneness before the Big Bang. The vastness of the sky is equaled by the vastness of the heart.

Neuroscience shows us that love is a necessity; its absence damages not only individuals, but also whole societies. Our brains require bonding and nurturing. Close emotional connection changes neural patterns, affecting our sense of self and making empathy possible. "In some important ways, people cannot be stable on their own," writes Thomas Lewis, MD, in *A General Theory of Love*.

The Beloved

All the work of Dante, the thirteenth- and fourteenth-century master poet of *The Divine Comedy*, was inspired by a single moment of love, and that love lives on. As Jungian analyst Robert Johnson describes, it began when the young Dante was standing near the Ponte Vecchio, a graceful medieval bridge that crosses the Arno River in Florence. It was just before 1300, and Dante spotted a young woman named Beatrice standing on the bridge. The sight of her ignited in him a vision that contained the whole of eternity. Dante only spoke to her a few times and, shortly after his epiphany, Beatrice died, carried off by the plague. Dante was stricken by the loss, but his work was inspired by Beatrice. She became his muse, his anima, the bridge between his soul and Heaven itself.

Six hundred fifty years later, during World War II, the Americans were chasing the German army up the Italian peninsula, as the Germans, in retreat, were blowing up everything in their wake, including bridges, to stop the Americans' progress. But no one wanted to blow up the Ponte Vecchio, because Beatrice had stood on it and Dante had written about her. So, the leaders of the German army made radio contact with the Americans and, in plain language, said they would leave the Ponte Vecchio intact if the Americans would promise not to use it. The promise held; the bridge was not blown up, and not one American soldier or piece of equipment went across it. The bridge was spared in a modern, ruthless war, because Beatrice had stood upon it and love had touched Dante.

Remember the days you were in love, how it felt on a spring day of crocuses and plum blossoms or a crisp autumn evening with the smell of burning leaves, how your heart soared as you met your Beatrice or Brent standing on the street corner. And if you never fell in love because of the oppression or pain around you, the Persian poet Rumi suggests, "Today is the day to start."

Love and spacious awareness are your true nature. They commingle. The sage Nisargadatta frames it this way: "Wisdom says I am nothing. Love says I am everything." Consciousness knows each experience; love connects it all. For a time, you can get caught in fear and separation. We all do. And then loving awareness remembers. Oh, this, too, is a place to love.

Love is inclusive, generous, and down-to-earth. Father Greg Boyle, author of *Tattoos on the Heart: The Power of Boundless Compassion,* writes about his work with gangs in LA's immigrant community. He also tends Dolores Mission Church, and in the 1980s, the church was a sanctuary for undocumented immigrants. Recently arrived men from Mexico and Central America would sleep each night in the church, and women and children in the convent. One morning, someone had angrily spray-painted across the front steps: WETBACK CHURCH, intended as a massive insult. Saddened and upset, Father Greg assured those inside, "I'll get one of the homies to clean it up later." It was one of the jobs the ex–gang kids he worked with would do.

But to his surprise, Petra Saldana, a normally quiet member of her church, stood up and addressed the congregation in no uncertain terms, "You will not clean this up! If there are people in our community who are despised and hated and left out because they are *mojados* (wetbacks) . . . then we shall proudly call ourselves a wetback church."

Solidarity. Compassion. Love.

Love's Many Faces

Love is unstoppable. It seeps into our words and our actions in a thousand ways. Sometimes it feels limited, sometimes expansive, but underneath, the mystery of love always pushes through. It has a thousand flavors. There is the kind of love expressed as desire: "I love chocolate ice cream; I'd love to find a new apartment." There is love as an exchange, businessman's love: "I'll love you if you make this deal." There is romantic love, the love that writes poetry and operas, that creates songs and tales of infatuation, falling in love, obsessive love, and the love like that for Helen of Troy, which launched a thousand ships and a war.

There is brotherly/sisterly love. This love cares for others, as part of the human family. In many cultures, family titles are used for everyone from politicians to Nobel laureates: Grandfather Tutu, Grandmother Angela Merkel. In America, we would say Auntie Hillary and Uncle Barack.

There is parental love for each precious child—unshakable caring, like the stories of mothers who lift cars to free their children and those of fathers who rush into burning buildings.

There is devotional love, and there is divine love, the spiritual ecstatic love that grows as vast as the ocean the moment you jump in.

And there is love for no reason, love in being alive, love married to invincible joy, openhearted and overflowing love, free and natural as a spring breeze.

When you open to any form of love, others feel it. Neuroscience calls this *limbic resonance*. Your mirror neurons and whole nervous system are constantly attuned to those around you, and love is communicable. We catch it from one another. Love permeates activity and changes all things. Neem Karoli Baba was asked how to get enlightened. "Love people" was his answer. "Love them and feed them."

Jerry Flaxstead, MD, describes his initial revulsion to a patient named Frank, an angry and obese homeless man who had diabetes, was unbathed, and had gangrenous legs and open sores. When he did not take his meds for his mental disorder, Frank would flail his arms and spew epithets and curses at those around him. Frank was admitted repeatedly to the hospital. For Dr. Flaxstead, Frank was a patient who was hard to love.

One day, Frank was brought to Richmond Hospital with congestive heart failure. The diagnosis was serious, and Dr. Flaxstead tended him as best as he could. Then twenty members of the down-home neighborhood church in whose shelter Frank sometimes slept arrived. They brought flowers and homemade food, chanted and sang hymns to Frank, creating a chorus of care and communion. When Dr. Flaxstead returned to Frank's room after tending to another patient on the ward, he saw that Frank was smiling, bathed in their love. The doctor realized that he had never really seen Frank at all.

Grace and Angst

No matter where we are, we can see the world through the eyes of love. Without love, everything is constrained, if not false. With love, we stand in the presence of all of life's mysteries. We can hold a golden apricot, a worn baseball glove, a photo of a child, or an old chipped cup, and our love can burst forth. Holding a stone, we feel the whole mountain. When we gaze at a pine tree, its presence becomes love of the earth itself. When love is present in us, the world returns our glance, radiant and filled with its blessings.

When Bill Moyers was filming *On Our Own Terms,* a PBS series on death and dying, he was concerned that his young production-crew members had never been close to death. So, he asked Frank Ostaseski, founder of Zen Hospice, to meet with the crew and describe the stages of dying and the people they would be filming. To humanize it, Frank handed out eight-by-ten black-and-white photos, intimate close-ups taken of patients who had come through the Zen Hospice over the years. The crew sat quietly meditating on the photos, looking at the eyes and tender faces of each individual facing death. After five minutes, Frank asked them to pass the photos to the person on their right, and they couldn't. They'd each fallen in love with the person whose photo they were holding.

The human heart longs to love and be loved, yet we are all too often afraid. We've been hurt, betrayed, abandoned, misunderstood, targeted, left out, and our love story has become a ghost story. The ghosts of loss and pain haunt us, warning us to hedge our bets and put up a shield to protect ourselves from further loss and rejection.

Rejection is one of the most difficult experiences to bear; it touches our most primal pains of abandonment, echoing the mistaken belief that there is something wrong with us, that we are unworthy, unattractive, unlovable. Whatever form our injury takes—family trauma, abuse, or neglect by an overwhelmed family or a loveless institution—we may become afraid to love. We have trouble opening to love, even for ourselves. Yet each of us is a mysterious, unique, amazing being, fully worthy of love.

Like rejection, fear of death or fear of the unknown can also block our love when we are afraid. We cling to a protective shell, a small sense of self that wants to be secure, to control life. We pretend we aren't vulnerable, but this is an illusion. We are incarnated in a delicate body, intertwined in the community of life. Our senses have evolved to be exquisitely attuned to the ever-changing world of pleasure and pain, sweet and sour, gain and loss. Love and freedom invite us to turn toward the full measure of this world. They offer the gifts of a flexible heart, wide enough to embrace experience, vulnerable yet centered.

"Ultimately it is upon your vulnerability that you depend," the poet Rilke writes. We are born and cared for by others, and we'll die in the same way. For the time that we are here, we are dependent on the web of life. We eat from the farmers' verdant fields, we trust other drivers to stay on their side of the road, we rely on the water department, the utility web, the electrical engineers, and the teachers, hospitals, and firefighters who sustain our lives. Listen to Mother Teresa: "If we have no peace, it's because we've forgotten we belong to each other." When we honor our vulnerability and our dependence on the community of life, we open to love.

Yes, you've been hurt and abandoned. But you found a way to survive your traumatic past and now the prison door is unlocked; you can walk out anytime. How long will you keep your heart closed? How long will you turn your back on love? Whatever blocks your love is, in the end, unreal. Take W. H. Auden's advice and learn to "love your crooked neighbor with your own crooked heart." Have courage. Tend to politics, care for the community around you, but remember that, in the end, it is your love that matters most. Love is your gateway to freedom and your last word.

Respond with Love

Ismael and Bridgit met in Indonesia and fell in love. She was working for an international nongovernmental organization, and he had just returned from a Fulbright Fellowship in America. They shared a devotion to the education of village children. Ismael came from a well-to-do business family who lived in Singapore and Brussels. Their clan was Sunni Muslim, well educated and devout. Bridgit had been raised with modern European ways, and Ismael's parents cringed when they first saw photos of her in a short sleeveless dress. Parents want their child to marry the person they think will bring happiness and success and will carry on the family's future. As if in a Shakespearean play, Ismael's parents did all they could to stop the relationship, threatening to cut off money and calling it a betrayal of the family. "They tried to stop us from loving each other," explained Bridgit. "All we wanted to do was to put more love in the world."

One night in London, she and Ismael looked at each other and lifted all the family-made suffering and fear up to the light. They drank tea, went for a walk under the stars, held each other. And they realized there was nothing wrong. For the first time, they knew they were not bound by the external opinions and judgments of others. All else—the ignorance and fears of the family—was superfluous. "We knew from within that we were allowed to love, we were right to love." They looked into their hearts and determined to respond with love.

They were married in a chapel in Scotland, and Ismael's parents attended. They had realized that their son would be their son no matter what. The minister read a passage on love and mercy from the Koran, and they all began to weep. It was a Brave New World, and Ismael and Bridgit knew they were free to love. They now have two beautiful children and work for the United Nations in Africa.

The Sparkle in Your Eyes

Romantic love can deepen when we let it. At first it is a kind of idol worship. It can come with idealism, possessiveness, jealousy, and need. Our songs and movies and dreams are full of idealistic, romantic love, the eros of sexual desire. "I want you, I need you, oh baby, oh baby." You see another person who matches enough of your inner image of "the desired one," your heartstrings resonate, and you are intoxicated, not only by his or her looks and wit and charm and strengths, but by how the person fits your own template of the one you want to love. The other person becomes, like Beatrice was for Dante, the ideal that awakens your own loving heart. You transfer onto the other person your longings, so he or she represents and carries beauty, strength, courage, intelligence, and steadiness. These qualities are also in you, but you don't always know it. They are unconscious, so your beloved becomes the carrier of your own golden qualities, and being with her or him helps you feel lovable, complete, whole.

You know the rest of the story. Placing your beloved on a pedestal works for a time, but slowly you look down from the golden glow and encounter the clay feet. They burp, belch, pout, get irritated, withdraw or cling, are too messy or too controlling. They become human. Of course, then you might discard the fallen lover and look for a better one, but this would be never-ending. Instead, when your idealistic love has been disappointed, a freer love is available. If you and the other person are a good-enough match, you can stay with the relationship and let it deepen and lead you to fuller, truer love. This is an invitation to love beyond expectations, clinging, or attachment.

Still, attachment, clinging, and expectations will arise along with love, and there will be times when your love is mixed with need and fear. Here is what you learn. Whenever you cling to how your partner (or your children or anyone) *should* be, you create suffering. Your partner does not want to be controlled; he or she wants to be loved, seen, accepted, held in your heart, and honored and respected and blessed by your love.

You might ask, if our love is not based on attachment, what holds us together? Care, commitment, and dedication. Commitment isn't about loving another person only when he does what you want, meets *your* needs, or when she fulfills your ideas for her life. You commit to love them as they are and dedicate yourself to their flowering. They will change and grow and explore, and sometimes they will do what you want and sometimes they won't. This is the paradox of love, that it does not grasp. Love is generous, spacious, and free to bless. We love best when we let go of expectations, just as we pray best when we don't expect a certain outcome. As T. S. Eliot instructs, "Teach us to care, and not to care."

"To have loved one soul is like adding its life to your own," said Meher Baba. True love, given freely, blesses the one you love and frees you at the same time. This is love that is openhearted, spontaneously offered, caring no matter what. Your commitment is to love, and your dedication is to honor the heart's connection.

Encounter with the Gods

Yale University surgeon and author Richard Selzer tells this story of love:

I stand by the bed where a young woman lies, her face post-operative, her mouth twisted in palsy, clownish. A tiny twig of the facial nerve, the one to the muscles of her mouth, has been severed. She will be thus from now on. The surgeon had followed with religious fervor the curve of her flesh; I promise you that. Nevertheless, to remove the tumor from her cheek, I had to cut the little nerve. Her young husband is in the room. He stands on the opposite side of the bed, and together they seem to dwell in the evening lamplight, isolated from me, private. Who are they, I ask myself, he and this wry-mouth I have made, who gaze at and touch each other so generously, greedily?

"Will my mouth always be like this?" she asks.

"Yes," I say, "it will be. It is because the nerve was cut."

She nods and is silent. But the young man smiles. "I like it," he says. "It's kind of cute."

All at once I know who he is. I understand, and I lower my gaze. One is not bold in an encounter with the gods. Unaware of my presence, he bends to kiss her crooked mouth, and I am so close I can see how he twists his own lips to accommodate her, to show her that their kiss still works. And I remember that in ancient Greece the gods appeared as mortals, and I hold my breath and let the wonder in.

Step out of the limitations that stop your love. Don't judge. Start just where you are. Honor every form of your love as a movement toward connection. Love mixed with desire is still seeking wholeness. Romantic love opens your heart to gaze upon another without fear or judgment. With love, learn to see the beauty of the one before you, and shine upon them. Then you can learn to shine the light of love back to yourself as well, not in a narcissistic, self-centered way, but treasuring yourself with respect and abiding appreciation. Love yourself.

Embodying Love

Look at your amazing, mysterious body in the mirror. Feel the love grow for your whole body—your nose, your eyes, your hair, your hands, your belly, your butt, your breasts, your stance. Eduardo Galeano writes:

> *The church says the body is sin.*
> *Science says the body is a machine.*
> *The marketplace says the body is good business.*
> *The body says, "I am a fiesta."*

Love being alive. Love your creative, distracted, overworked mind. Love your anxiety and depression and longing and wisdom. Love your food, celebrate your survival, open your senses to the mysterious communion of life right where you are.

Love the natural world. Like Annie Dillard, who has spent her life walking the hills "looking for the tree with lights in it," you will have moments when you see the sacred shine from quivering aspen, autumnal maples, or textured clouds, the sunlight of heaven piercing the veil and illuminating everyday forms like a Michelangelo masterpiece. Love the creatures of the world, the complex web of teeming earthworms, bacteria, bees, and beasts that live and die in an incalculable process of re-creation on this cooled piece of star. Start anywhere. Love dogs, cats, dolphins, squirrels, mockingbirds, lizards, elephants. Love men and women, tribes, nations, the unending varieties of human character and theater. Love is a sacred wellspring that never runs out. The freedom of love is based on the perennial renewal of love itself; it actually can grow. It is this simple: your whole life is a curriculum of love.

Love Baked Fresh

Some people learn love spontaneously when their children are born. Some when their children are in trouble. Some learn from falling in love, from caring for the one they're with. Though your True Nature is love and awareness, at times you forget, which is utterly human. Ursula Le Guin reminds us, "Love must be remade each day, baked fresh like bread."

Modern neuroscience reinforces that while love is native to us, it is also a quality that can be developed. Like gratitude and forgiveness, love can be invited, nourished, and awakened. It can flower and expand. It can become our way, no matter what. Every great spiritual tradition understands this. Ecstatic music and art, devotional prayer, sacred rituals, and contemplative practices all offer us ways to open to love. Neuroscience shows how practices of love and compassion can change our nervous system and greatly increase access to these capabilities.

Practices of lovingkindness and compassion drawn from Eastern psychology are being adapted for medicine, education, psychotherapy, conflict resolution, even for business. The inner trainings of meditation and prayer tune us in to the love channel. They invite us into the reality of love over and over until the time comes when love bursts our heart open, swoops in and fills us, and we can't say no.

Think of those who choose love in this world, and remember that you can awaken your own love and join them. Practicing in any of these ways profoundly affects how you hold others. Thupten Jinpa, His Holiness the Dalai Lama's translator, tells a story of a middle-aged doctor of internal medicine who came to their Stanford program on lovingkindness and mindful compassion. The doctor was disheartened. He had lost his spark at work and felt weary and pressured by the speed of care required by the insurance-driven medical system. After two months of compassion and kindness classes, he said he changed the way he greeted his patients and listened to and interacted with them. Meditating on lovingkindness and compassion renewed his sense of connection to himself and those he treated. One of his patients, an older woman, asked him, "Doctor, you seem different, what has happened to you? Are you in love or something?"

Blessing of Respect

Love brings with it the blessing of respect. At a men's retreat, Richard shared with other attendees a story about his role as the host of a Sunday afternoon radio show in Los Angeles that was devoted to the blues. He got lots of mail, including from devoted listeners incarcerated in Southern California prisons. One letter came from an older man, Walter Jones, who requested he play some of the early blues greats: Blind Lemon Jefferson, Muddy Waters, and Big Joe Williams. Richard devoted part of one Sunday show to these blues icons, announcing they'd been requested by a Mr. Walter Jones, a man who clearly had rich knowledge of the history of the blues. Several weeks later he received a letter from Walter in prison, thanking him for the show and the acknowledgment, adding, "That's the first time I ever remember hearing my name spoken with respect."

When Yasim, a refugee from Kosovo, came to the United States at age seventeen, she was disoriented and lost, filled with anxiety and worry. She studied health technology in a community college and got a job in a large, overbusy urban clinic. With the ongoing stress in the health-care system, she felt overwhelmed.

She attended a weekend retreat and learned *metta* (lovingkindness) meditation. Her meditations were naturally visual and filled with colors, and she was able to apply this newfound skill to her daily work. As each patient arrived, Yasim would sense a color that surrounded them, then in her mind's eye she would fill that color with love. This helped her see beyond each patient's demeanor— their worn clothes, illness, or mood—and hold them in her heart. But love for herself was more difficult for her. Her family in Kosovo, when they were trying to survive, had been very harsh, and the legacy was painful. She was doubtful, self-critical, filled with shame. When she thought of her friends or the patients at the clinic, each came with a color. But when she directed thoughts of love toward herself, she found only a hard, black hole in her heart.

One day, she received an affectionate message from a work colleague. This was a woman Yasim had a secret crush on. The note filled her heart with waves of kindness and a golden color. Another note brought more joy. When Yasim meditated and tried metta for herself, the black hole dissolved into open spaciousness and the colors of luminous clouds appeared. She told me, "Loving others healed half my heart; feeling loved helped heal the other half." Being human, Yasim had to repeat the practice. Openness doesn't always last. The heart opens and closes, and feelings fade. But now Yasim knows what it's like to feel loved and to love herself.

Trust in your goodness. Find the safety you need to open. Let love resurrect you. Let its magnetic pull connect you with the life energy you were born into. Let love make you quiet, tender, strong, and caring. Let love make you dance. Discover the love that is your home. Live from the love that you *are*.

PRACTICE

Lovingkindness Meditation

I am larger than I thought!
I did not know I held so much goodness!

—WALT WHITMAN

Begin the practice of lovingkindness by meditating for fifteen or twenty minutes in a quiet place. Sit so that you feel comfortable. Let your body rest and your heart be soft.

It is best to begin by directing lovingkindness to those you love, because often people can find it difficult to direct love to themselves. Picture someone you love a lot, where love comes easily and is uncomplicated. Start where it's easy to first open the heart. You can even begin with a child or a pet.

Breathe gently and recite inwardly the following traditional good wishes directed toward their well-being.

May you be filled with lovingkindness.
May you be safe.
May you be well.
May you be at ease and happy.

As you repeat these phrases, hold this loved one in lovingkindness. Adjust the words and images to best open your heart. Repeat these phrases and kind intentions over and over again, letting the feelings permeate your body and mind.

This meditation may, at times, feel mechanical or awkward. It can also bring up feelings of irritation or anger. If this happens, it is especially important to be patient and kind toward yourself, allowing whatever arises to be held in a spirit of friendliness and kind affection.

After a few minutes, picture a second easy person and extend the same wishes of lovingkindness to them. Whether the image or feelings are clear or not does not matter. Simply continue to plant the seeds of loving wishes, repeating the phrases gently, no matter what arises. The rule in lovingkindness practice is to follow the way that most easily opens your heart.

Now after a time, you are ready to turn to lovingkindness for yourself. Envision or imagine these two loved ones gazing back at you with the same well wishing. They want you, too, to be held in kindness, to be safe and well, to be happy. Picture them saying to you, kindly:

May you be filled with lovingkindness.
May you be safe.
May you be well.
May you be at ease and happy.

Receive these gratefully. After a few repetitions, take their good wishes into yourself. You may even wish to place a hand on your heart. And recite:

May you be filled with lovingkindness.
May you be safe.
May you be well.
May you be at ease and happy.

When you have established a sense of lovingkindness for yourself, you can expand your meditation to include others. Choose a benefactor, someone in your life who has loved or cared for you. Picture this person and carefully recite the same phrases.

When lovingkindness for your benefactor has developed, you can gradually include other people you care about in your meditation. Picture each beloved person, recite the same phrases, evoking a sense of lovingkindness for each person in turn. After this, you can include a wider circle of friends. Then gradually extend your meditation step-by-step to picture and include community members, neighbors, people everywhere, animals, all beings, the whole earth.

Finally, include the difficult people in your life, even your enemies, wishing that they, too, may be filled with loving-kindness and peace. This will take practice. But as your heart opens, first to loved ones and friends, you will find that in the end, you won't want to close it to anyone.

Lovingkindness can be practiced anywhere. You can use this meditation in traffic jams, in buses, and on airplanes. As you silently practice this meditation among people, you will immediately feel a wonderful connection with them: the power of lovingkindness. It will calm your mind, open your heart, and keep you connected to all beings.

Chapter 3

Trusting the Living Universe

*You can pick all the flowers but
you can't stop the spring.*

—PABLO NERUDA

We are not the small self our worries believe us to be. We are life renewing itself again and again. Trust knows that nothing real can be lost. Whenever I would go to my teacher Ajahn Chah to speak about some experience I felt to be important—a terrible fever, a luminous meditation—or some worry for the fate of the world, he would smile like a grandfather being shown sandcastles by his three-year-old and remind me, "If you hold on to any expectation, you miss the wisdom. It is impermanent. Be the One Who Knows, the witness to it all. This is how trust grows." And it is how love grows as well. Trust and love are the keys.

Tending Our Garden

Maria had a small stroke the same year her husband was laid off work and her son entered treatment for meth addiction. She felt like the biblical Job. Though she got disability payments, she was afraid they'd lose their home. As her teacher, I guided her to work with the practices of trust and present-moment awareness. She used prayer beads to focus her mind, especially during her months of rehabilitation, and recited, "Rest in the present. Heal in the present. Trust."

As she and her son gradually recovered, she practiced self-care and attended Al-Anon meetings. After a long, difficult time, she healed, her husband got his job back, and her son completed a year in rehab and is so far clean and sober. "Without trust, I would never have made it," she confided.

We are part of a vast plan of life unfolding. When individual loss strikes, or there is a communal trauma, it is not a mistake. We have what it takes to endure it with courage. We can survive and grow strong, like the wild trees on mountain ridges that have weathered storms and become beautiful. With trust, we plant our seeds, tend them, and discover that although it isn't possible to control the world, we can always care for the garden of our life.

Trust is empowering. I think of the Norwegian pastor who worked secretly underground during World War II, saving Jews, gays, Gypsies, all of whose lives were threatened by the Nazis. He was called into Gestapo headquarters and told to sit in the metal chair opposite a German officer. After turning on a harsh lamp, the interrogation officer took out of his holster a Luger and placed the pistol on the desk between himself and the pastor. Without a moment's hesitation, the pastor reached into his satchel and placed his Bible on the desk next to the German Luger. The officer demanded, "Why did you do that?" The pastor replied, "You put your weapon on the table and so have I." With trust in the rightness of his choices, the minister withstood the long interrogation and, undaunted, returned to his church and his dangerous work.

Take a moment to reflect on trust. How would it feel to live with wise trust, with the sense that things will somehow work out, perhaps not in the way you think they should, but in some magnificent way? Notice your body relax, your heart ease. Rumi instructs, "Pretend the universe is rigged in your favor." For Gandhi, trust emerged from this same timeless vision. "When I despair," he wrote, "I remember that all through history, the way of truth and love has always won. Yes, there have been murderers and tyrants, and for a time they can seem invincible. But in the end, they always fall. Think of it, always."

During hard times, trust demands a shift from the small self, the body of fear, to a connection with that which is vast, sacred, holy. It is a trust in the greatness of the human spirit.

Enduring the pain of broken trust, it may take some time until your faith in life is restored. But it can be renewed. Remember, it is not just you. We've all been betrayed, had our trust broken, abused. Sometimes betrayal starts in a painful childhood. Sometimes it is later: lovers who had affairs, business partners who betrayed and stole from you, family members fighting, strangers who violate your home or body, institutions that lie. These breaches of trust are difficult to heal. But you can learn to trust again. Wise trust is not naïve. You can be trusting and protect your body, your heart, and your possessions. Wise trust requires discernment, the ability to distinguish what is worthy of trust and, most of all, the ways you have to trust yourself.

We can trust that the joy and the suffering given to us are what we need to awaken to freedom. Hardship and loss are the graduate school of trust. They teach us survival and a freedom that is unshakable. There is a force born in us from a thousand generations of ancestors, survivors who have offered us life. Now it's our turn. Even when we've lost money, our job, a relationship, or hope, it is not the end. Like the grass that pushes through cracks in the sidewalk, trust can grow again. No matter how lost or desolate we may feel, something new awaits us, and life continues.

The Dance of Life

We live in a culture that encourages the belief that we can control everything. We try to eat healthy diets, watch the Weather Channel for storm predictions 24/7, and stand in long security lines at airports. But, ultimately, no one can predict illness, tornadoes, or accidents. Nor can we accurately predict rainbows, smiles, gestures of love, or the span of a life. Our politicians foster fear, often misleading us about impending danger, putting out one fearful story after another. We were once directed to fear Communists, nuclear war, and gays; now we are encouraged to fear terrorists, immigrants, and Muslims.

H. L. Mencken, a journalist in the 1920s, saw this whipping-up of fear as endemic to politics. "The whole aim of politics is to keep the populace alarmed—and hence clamorous to be led to safety—by menacing it with an endless series of hobgoblins, almost all of them imaginary." This dynamic persists today. A barrage of scary stories and lies from politicians and officials resonates with our underlying anxiety.

Yes, things are uncertain, but wisdom brings us love, perspective, and the ability to trust. Wisdom invites us to live with a trusting heart. Howard Zinn, author of the celebrated *People's History of the United States*, notes, "Revolutionary change comes as an endless succession of surprises." He cites the fall of the Soviet Union, the Spanish shift from fascism to democracy, the Chinese Communist turn toward capitalism.

I keep encountering young people who, in spite of all the evidence of terrible things happening, also give hope. There are hundreds of thousands working for the good everywhere . . . To be hopeful in hard times is not just foolishly romantic. It is based on the fact that human history is a history not only of cruelty but also of compassion, sacrifice, courage, kindness. What we choose to emphasize in this complex history will determine our lives. If we see only the worst, it destroys our capacity to do something. If we remember those times and places—and there are so many—where people have behaved magnificently, this gives us the energy to act, and at least the possibility of sending this spinning top of a world in a different direction. The future is an infinite succession of presents, and to live now as we think human beings should live, in defiance of all that is bad around us, is itself a marvelous victory.

What is true for the collective is true for each of us. In the worst of times, you may lose your job or your home, become seriously ill, or find yourself in a painful divorce. Yet the heart can still trust—even in the midst of your difficulty. This is not naïve trust—you are not necessarily counting on a particular outcome, such as finding a better job or even getting well. The heart can trust in the timeless spirit behind this magnificent dance.

We can't know how life will turn out. Sometimes a painful process leads to an unexpectedly better circumstance later. Sometimes it doesn't and becomes a difficult lesson for your soul to learn. It's all the music of life, and all is workable. With wise trust, your heart can be free wherever you are.

Wise Trust

When Alvaro's father died, his six siblings fought, two of them with lies and greed, to gain control of the family construction company. In two years, they nearly robbed Alvaro of his inheritance. But they were his family, parents of beloved nieces and nephews. He had been with them for every family gathering—weddings, holidays, *quinceañeras*. Family was his life. Alvaro went through shock and loss, anger, grief, and tears. After a year, he realized how he could trust his siblings again: he could only trust them to be themselves. He did not want them to colonize his heart or his life with anger and resentment. He told his lawyer to use every legal means to protect his inheritance. But he would not give up loving them. By seeing them clearly, he regained a trust in himself. And through sometimes painful legal battles, he learned he could care for himself and come to trust in a new and wiser way.

The best forms of healing, therapy, and meditation are all about learning to trust. This trust is the genuine kind. Your child is in trouble, your job is insecure, you worry about how you will get by, you are haunted by painful trauma from the past. But this is not the end of the story.

Working with combat veterans returning from Iraq and Afghanistan, and other men who had experienced violence and trauma, my colleagues Michael Meade, Luis Rodriguez, and I created retreats in a lodge deep in the redwood forest. There, the men are free to give voice to longings and terrors, loves and losses. They tell their untold stories and participate in ceremonies created to welcome them back into the community. On one retreat, the men's days were filled with activities to connect them with themselves and with one another. They practiced creative writing and poetry, and engaged in song, ritual, and martial arts. They learned the myths and songs of returning warriors—African, Mayan, Irish, Tibetan—which called out for mercy, understanding, and solace. Each evening, the old stone-and-redwood lodge was lit by candles, and the men were invited to stand and tell their stories.

One night TJ, the youngest there, who had been in a Los Angeles street gang, spoke up. Voice shaking, he described the scene of fighting between Crips and Bloods, of a slow-moving car from the projects, and a drive-by shooting that had killed a friend just the week before. When the rival gang started firing, TJ ran, but his younger friend was too slow and got hit and killed. As soon as he could, TJ ran back to hold his buddy, fending off the police who had come to the crime scene. He wept as he wondered aloud if he could have done anything more to save his friend.

Rudy, a burly ex-Marine recently returned from Iraq, moved over to put his tattooed arm around TJ's shoulder and told him, "You did the right thing. When the firefight starts, you have to get down. But you never leave your man."

After an emotional silence, Rudy spoke of his own experiences: "I can't tell you what I saw. But worse, I can't tell you what I had to do." His eyes moist, Rudy went on to describe an evening in Anbar when he was guarding a checkpoint at twilight. A group of Iraqis approached. He ordered them to stop for a search, as there had been recent suicide bombings. One older man continued coming. Rudy shouted, "Stop! Stop!" in both English and Arabic, but the man just kept moving toward the compound gate. Rudy opened fire and the man fell. The Iraqi women in the group began screaming and shouting. A translator said to Rudy, "Couldn't you tell? The old man was deaf."

Rudy and TJ wept together. And then, in the candlelight under the dark redwoods, a hundred men stood up and began to sing the haunting melody of African warriors returning home. For half an hour, they surrounded Rudy and TJ with their deep, sonorous voices, and little by little sang them back into their bodies. Today,

Rudy works in a project mentoring young men who are leaving the gang life.

You, too, can be haunted by the unfinished traumas of your life until you find a way to come to terms with them. You can do this in many ways, through meditation and therapy, art and community, ritual and taking time to heal. Gradually you'll learn that freedom does not mean that your painful experiences go away. Instead they become like the battle scars that decorate the body of a Masai warrior, the stretch marks on a woman's belly, the hard-won secret medicines gained along the great journey. The traumas change from a locked-in response or fearful habit to a tender, instructive memory. They become the fuel for the flame of life to burn more brightly in your heart.

Beyond Despair

Your suffering is not the end of the story. It doesn't have to define you. The poet Rumi's tomb says:

Come, come, whoever you are.
Wanderer, worshipper, lover of life.
Though you have broken your vow a hundred times,
Ours is not a caravan of despair.

Whether it is others who break their vows or we who have broken ours, Rumi reminds us that we can carry on, not in despair, but with a deeper trust. Trust begins in the innocence of the child, ready to step into the arms of even the most unfit parent. Then come life's disillusionments and measure of suffering. This is not a mistake. Loss and betrayal are woven into the fabric of life, the inevitable limits of human incarnation. Outer losses turn us back to seek what is truly trustworthy. From disillusion can grow compassion and a bigger perspective. With these, trust arises again, deeper and wiser.

Keith, a student of Tibetan Buddhism, came to see me. He had undertaken the traditional Vajrayana practice of 100,000 prostrations, and with each bow he took refuge in the Buddha and his teachings. But his lama had gone back to Nepal and wouldn't be returning until the following year. After beginning with a few thousand prostrations, Keith was stuck. Now, each time he started to bow, his body hurt, his feelings would turn to stone, and he could hardly force himself to do even one more prostration. We talked about his practice. I said that one of the purposes of a repeated practice like bowing is purification and explained that as he bowed, any underlying physical, emotional, and mental patterns that might block his wholehearted dedication and devotion would naturally arise. These are where deep transformations take place.

I suggested that we bow together and see what happened. We stood side by side ready to bow and take refuge in the Buddha and his teachings. I asked Keith to be especially mindful of his body. He found himself suddenly cold, shivering, and fearful. He stayed with these feelings and they grew stronger. I started to bow, and as he began to move, his throat tightened, his heart pounded. I had him close his eyes and notice all the feelings. Then I simply asked him how old he felt. His eyes began to tear and his voice was quivering as he started to speak. "I am six years old." "And what has happened?" I asked. A story poured out how his father, the parent who most loved and protected Keith, was carried off to the hospital with a major heart attack. This left Keith with a crying baby brother and an abusive, bipolar mother. When his father came home from the hospital a month later, he was not the same man. The heart attack had left him sick and broken. He faded and died within a few years. All of Keith's sense of well-being and hope was dashed by his father's illness. He no longer felt protected or cared for.

"How does this connect with bowing?" I asked, as we stood together. He shook his head and said, "After my father was gone, I gave up. My childhood became so hard, I concluded that life is just untrustworthy. I'm afraid to take refuge in anything, because it can be snatched away in a second, like my father."

I asked him to imagine holding the six-year-old child who was abandoned, tenderly and with great compassion. Then, after a time, I looked him in the eyes and asked, "Is this scared six-year-old who you really are?" He understood that he'd been carrying an unconscious fear for years. Now he could see that he was no longer a child, and that he'd lived and survived the pain of his father's loss. Keith realized he could start to trust again and live life here and now. When he was ready, Keith and I stood up and we bowed together. Later, he completed his 100,000 bows, beautifully.

Embraced by a Living Universe

Human incarnation is mysterious because it ends. Death will come to you and wipe the slate, no matter who you are, no matter how small or great your accomplishments. "The graveyards are full of indispensable men," noted the French general Charles de Gaulle. How do we live with the fact of death, the final mystery? It can paralyze us or we can turn toward it, bow to its presence, and live freely.

Fear can be wildly irrational. Our primitive brain fears sharks, terrorists, airline crashes. In the past year, there were fewer than thirty unprovoked shark attacks in the United States and 4.5 million dog bites. Seventeen Americans were killed by terrorist attacks, and 36,000 died of the flu. You are a hundred times more likely to die in a car crash than in an airplane. We scare ourselves. Our fear of sharks, terrorists, and falling planes is mostly imaginary. As Helen Keller explained, "Security is mostly a superstition. It does not exist in nature, nor do children as a whole experience it. Avoiding danger is no safer in the long run than outright exposure. Life is either a daring adventure or nothing."

Rosina, a mother of two boys, ages seven and ten, came to work with me. She had breast cancer that had metastasized extensively. Although she was undertaking treatment, her chances of living more than a few months were slim. She tried practicing living mindfully in the moment, but her agitation and fear were strong. With some guidance, she came into her body, holding the knots, constriction, and panic with kindness. Still, the pain of the cancer was debilitating, and she was terrified of entering the black hole of death and leaving her children.

As we met regularly, Rosina learned to hold all these intense feelings and sensations with compassion. She cried and shook and felt waves of terror. Slowly, she found some calm, and eventually she was able to embrace all of her emotions and feelings. She understood that we don't get to choose when we die.

One day, with my encouragement, she let herself open to her greatest fear, the abyss of death. As she did, she felt herself falling, trying to hold on, then letting go and falling into infinite blackness. To her surprise, the endless dark space became soft, black velvet with a background of shining stars. Her expression transformed to one of wonder and relief as she opened to this mystery, to a trust bigger than her fears, and she could feel herself being held by a living universe.

Janice struggled with frequent bouts of fear. I asked her to keep a journal and become exquisitely aware of each time her patterns of worry, fear, or self-judgment arose. But the more she paid attention, the more distraught she became. She recorded an unrelenting stream of worries and feelings of failure. Then, reviewing her notes, she saw her unremitting suffering clearly. She wept and her heart softened.

After allowing herself to feel the sadness and grief over her life, she got curious and asked herself, "What is going on that makes me suffer so much?" Spontaneously, an image arose of herself as a frightened little girl, trying her best to hold it together. When she was young, her family lost their home, and her parents, who fought and blamed each other, got increasingly angry and controlling with Janice and her brother. When she was alone as a child, Janice would put a puppet of a demon on her hand, and it would shout out her fears and berate her. Suddenly she realized that the demon had, misguidedly, been trying to protect her. "But, oh my, forty years later, and I'm still doing this to myself!"

Insecurity is wired into the older levels of our brain. The primitive brain is always on alert for trouble, but that is not necessarily wisdom or trust. Wisdom invites us to live with a trusting heart. With awareness and compassion, we can release our fear. With trust, we can put down the demons of fear and insecurity and allow the unfolding of life. With a trusting heart, we become both loving and detached, combining serenity and care, open to whatever comes.

A Sufi master known for his open-mindedness died in the fullness of time and found himself outside the gates of Heaven. There an angel said, "Go no further, O mortal, until you have proven your worthiness to enter into Paradise!" The master responded, "Just a minute. First, can you prove this is really Heaven and not just the wishful fantasy of my disordered mind undergoing death?" Before the angel could reply, a voice from inside the gates shouted, "Let him in. He's one of us!" What does this mean? Look deeply at the notion of death you carry. Those you know who have died, are they gone or do their spirits live on? Are they lost to you, or do you carry them within? The founder of modern chemistry, Antoine Lavoisier, discovered, "All is transformed, nothing is lost." How do you hold this mystery?

Aging with Trust

In every cycle and vocation of life, we have to relearn the art of trust. Every night we die, trusting in the oblivion of sleep, and we awaken the next morning reborn to fresh sunlight. Like the seasons, we are moved from one cycle to the next. Instead of struggling against change, we might as well make them a dance.

Joan Baez and her ninety-two-year-old mom sang for my sixtieth Birthday Ball, which was also my daughter's twenty-first birthday, her coming of age. I was dressed in a tux and feeling at the top of my game. Now, a decade later, when I look in the mirror I see a balding guy in pretty good shape for his seventy-first year. But I also feel the gradual waning of strength, memory, and capacity that is the natural process of the aging body. When I feel wise and gracious, I see that aging is just natural. It's what bodies do in the last chapters of this incarnation. And then I go through periods of denial, ignoring, or struggling against the stream of life. I don't mean to discount the value of healthy living to stay active and fit, but the decline is real and inevitable.

You can choose to resist or be gracious. If you age without trust, you will contract and suffer, already turning toward death. Your heart will not be free to love and enjoy each day, to dance with life.

As for me, the game isn't over, it's just changed. I want to serve the world and live in it with trust, love, and full presence to the last. This is the great invitation—to live with a trusting heart. This is our freedom. The greatest Zen masters say, "Enlightenment is fulfilled by the trusting heart."

PRACTICE
Trust in the Big Picture

Sit quietly. Sense how your body breathes 15,000 breaths a day, your heart pumps 90,000 times a day, your senses and digestion all operate in a completely trustworthy manner. Now look around at the earth, the plants, the trees, and remember the cycling of the days and the turning of the seasons, the sparkling stars wheeling above as the world turns. Relax. Sense a trust that you are part of something vast, an unfolding of life itself. You are part of a long chain of humans, part of something great. The lineage of life brought you this human birth. It will carry you through the ups and downs, for years and years. Breathe deep in the rhythms of life. Relax. Trust.

PRACTICE
Trust Your Inner Knowing

Learn to trust your body. Begin by mindfully and lovingly feeling what is going on in your body. Sense the state of your body today, its signals and needs. Listen carefully to what your body has to say to you. What healing does it want? What care? What wisdom does it have to offer you? Your body has been waiting for your attention. Trust it. Even if you have been out of touch for a long time, you can regain confidence step-by-step by trusting your bodily experience.

Just as you can listen to your body, you can learn to trust your intuition and instincts. Consider any situation or problem. What do your instincts tell you? Pause. Listen deeply. Below the level of stories, of habits, and of immediate reactions are deeper levels of knowing—feeling, intuition, conscience, and care. Take time to tune in mindfully, with respect. Let self-confidence and trust in your intuition grow.

Discover that loving awareness is big enough to hold all of your experience. Let confidence and resilience grow from training your loving mindfulness. You can be aware of whatever is present, you can relax and trust yourself to surf on the ever-changing waves of life.

PRACTICE
Be Inspired by Trust

Take inspiration from those who live with trust, those with a positive spirit even in hard times.

Here's how: bring to mind a few people you know who inspire you with their trust.

Notice what it is like when a person lives with trust instead of anxiety. See how they carry themselves. Sense the uplifting effect they have on others. Envision yourself becoming more trusting like them. Picture moving through your day with confidence and trust, relaxed and present.

Now, remember the times you have felt your own healthy sense of trust, confidence and strength, a love that was not afraid. This trust is within you. Wise trust is not naïve, it sees clearly that some people are not trustworthy, but this does not destroy the overall spirit of trust. It is trust in yourself and life itself.

Invite your trust to grow, live with it.

Trust is the gateway to happiness.

Chapter 4

The Eternal Present

To see a World in a Grain of Sand
And a Heaven in a Wild Flower,
Hold Infinity in the palm of your hand
And Eternity in an hour.

—WILLIAM BLAKE

Eternity is here, always alive in the present moment. Mindfulness invites us to return to now, the present moment, instead of being buried in thoughts of a past that no longer exists or fantasizing about a future that is yet to come. In the present moment, we learn to see clearly and kindly. With the power of mindfulness, we can become fully present to the unbearable beauty and the inevitable tragedy that comprise our human life. We can honorably embrace and tend the life we've been given.

Touching the Eternal Present

My friend, writer and humorist Anne Lamott, describes encountering the timeless present in Tibetan practice. "I have a recording of a Tibetan nun singing a mantra of compassion over and over for an hour, eight words repeated over and over, and every line feels different, feels cared about and experienced fully as she is singing. You never once have the sense that she is glancing down at her watch, thinking, 'Jesus Christ, it's only been fifteen minutes.' Forty-five minutes later she is still singing each line distinctly, word by word until the last word is sung." Mostly, things are not that simple and pure, with attention to each syllable as life sings itself through us. Yet this kind of attention is the prize.

Stories of great masters may make us ask, "How can I be like them?" In response, each master might invite you to the reality of the present in his or her own way. Ajahn Chah would say, "Let go and become awareness itself. Be the One Who Knows." Dipa Ma would say, "Love and be at peace no matter what." Suzuki Roshi would say, "Just be exactly where you are. Instead of waiting for the bus, realize you are on the bus." Thich Nhat Hanh would say, "Rest in mindfulness, this moment, the eternal present." The Tibetan Dzogchen masters agree: "Enlightenment is not far away. It is freedom here and now, to be tasted whenever you open to it."

Robert Aitken Roshi was the senior Western Zen Master who taught in America. Just before his retirement, he attended a meeting of nearly a hundred Western Buddhist teachers. In a beautiful talk, he spoke of his love of Dharma and his life of practice, including his first Zen encounter with R. H. Blyth, an Englishman who taught in Japan, became a noted translator of haiku, and was interned as an enemy alien in a Japanese prison camp. Aitken Roshi reflected on years of leading *sesshin* and teaching koans. He also described the difficult time he had with his own doubts even after he had begun to teach as a Zen Roshi. He was known for his sympathy for all Zen students in their difficult studies.

One of the meditation teachers present asked him for a final gift: Would Roshi be willing to tell us the answer to a Zen koan? In response, Aitken Roshi described an early encounter with his Zen teacher Nyogen Senzaki in New York City. Senzaki held up a large pottery bowl with a spiral painted from the inside center to the edge. The koan Senzaki asked him was, "Which way does the spiral go, from the inside out or the outside in?"

"What is the answer?" asked one of the teachers in the crowd. It was the end of Roshi's talk and he had been sitting motionless for one and a half hours. Nearly eighty, he stood up slowly, wobbling. Then he extended his arms, hands upward. He turned his whole body around, first one way, then the other way. Inside out and outside in. His answer was this. He became the bowl; he was the spiral itself.

Notice Now

A few years ago, I had the pleasure of leading a retreat with Thich Nhat Hanh. He called his teaching that day "No Death, No Fear" and told the story of awakening from a dream in which he was having a conversation with his beloved mother a year after she had passed away. He'd been close with her, and after her death he grieved the loss terribly. But on a moonlit night in his mountain hermitage in Vietnam, he awoke from a dream of his mother, fully feeling the reality of her presence. "I understood," he said, "that my mother never died." He could hear her voice inside himself. He went outside, and she became the moonlight tenderly caressing his skin. As he walked barefoot among the tea plants, he was able to feel her with him. The idea that she was gone simply wasn't true. He realized his feet were "our" feet, he said, and "together my mother and I were leaving footprints in the damp evening soil."

Like Thich Nhat Hanh, Isabella had to embrace life and death in each moment. Her two children, born a year apart, both had cystic fibrosis. Their life expectancy was limited, their bodies wracked by coughs. By the time they were in high school, the genetic disorder had filled their lungs with sticky mucus. Nicolas was a geek, a brilliant teen web designer; Daniella was an athlete, a volleyball player with great dexterity. Maybe with the miracle of a lung transplant, they would live until age thirty. Looking at them could break your heart.

We all know we will die, but for Isabella, her children's every cough or stomach pain was a jolt, a reminder of their mortality. When Isabella came to me to learn mindfulness, she was desperate "to stop her mind's incessant living in the future." As she began to meditate, she was horrified to see how often fears filled her mind and how little she noticed where she was. It took weeks of hard work, a thousand times redirecting her attention, and gradually Isabella began to notice her morning meal, the pink oleander at the corner, the hiss of the water sprinkler, the blue floral tablecloth. Step-by-step it began to work, and relief slowly came into her heart. She opened to the day's sunset, to the old woman seated on the porch next door, to the simple nourishment of each moment.

"My refuge is the present. At first, mindfulness was a way out of inner torment. But now it is a way of life. None of us knows the number of our days and our destiny. We have to live here or we miss everything. I want to be here for every moment of my children's life. And mine, too."

As Jon Kabat-Zinn says, "The little things, the little moments? They aren't little." Even your difficulties can be better tended by staying here and now.

To become free of the tyranny of time, become interested in the present. Notice the experience of now with its measure of joys and sorrows. Relax into now; it is your home. As you take care to live now, you will discover that it covers the whole of time. Just this moment—as you read this page—pause and reflect on your plans for the day. Notice that you are here, now, envisioning plans. You can plan and remember, but it all happens now.

Moral Mathematics of the Moment

Freedom is always found just where you are. Whether you are caring for a child, building a business, playing a game, or healing an illness, it all takes place right now. Hurrying and worrying don't bring more time. All we truly ever have is the present moment. The past is gone; the future is not yet here. The art of living is to *be* in the eternal present, open to what is. It takes only a moment to break the spell of time, to step out of our thoughts and see the sunlight reflecting on the windowpane, taste the dazzling mystery of a tangerine or a shrimp.

So much of modern life feels rushed. Look at the mystery of time. We are pressed for time, stuck in traffic, late for a meeting, our minds filled with tasks ahead or past mistakes. Yet time is created by thoughts, ideas about times other than now. Of course, time consciousness has great value. It allows the mystery to be remembered, organized, planned for, and learned from. But mostly living in thoughts of other times causes stress and anxiety. Focusing too much on the past and future dims the vibrancy of the present.

In 2007, the *Washington Post* conducted an experiment in "context, perception, and priorities." The newspaper had world-famous violinist Joshua Bell take his Stradivarius into a morning DC Metro (subway) station and play complex, gorgeous Preludes by Bach. A thousand commuters passed by, yet almost no one stopped to listen, except for a few children. The *Post* called it "the moral mathematics of the moment." People were in a hurry and focused elsewhere, and Bell's hat filled with a total of $32 in change, a portion of one ticket to his Kennedy Center performance the next night. How often have you or I rushed through life lost in thought, missing the violin and the simple miracles that are here in every moment?

Wherever you are, whatever you are doing, stop. Take a breath. Freedom comes alive whenever you are present and not lost in thought. When you are fully with your children, your lover, your garden, your work, your own body, you come alive. Centered in the present, you can also plan, consider, direct your life more effectively. When you are *here,* you see with greater clarity and respond with genuine love. There comes a growing capacity to accept and embrace what is here now with a courageous heart.

Beginner's Mind

Paul traveled often for his marketing company, but was a hands-on father at home. His oldest daughter, Stella, at fourteen was maturing, but his seven- and nine-year-old, Joshua and Callie, were fighting, insulting, hitting, and teasing each other. On drives, the backseat was a battle zone with cries of "She started it!" "No! He did it first." Paul worried that they'd never grow out of this and would end up adult siblings who hated each other.

Returning home from overseas one day, tired and jet-lagged, Paul took the two youngest on a drive to see his sister. As they began fighting, he yelled at them to stop, but they only continued pinching and teasing each other in a stealthier way. They pulled over for a bathroom stop, and as Callie rushed to get out of the car, she tripped over the curb and fell hard on her elbow, scraping her face. Paul got a cloth and antiseptic to wipe off the blood and tend her face, and Joshua ran inside to get ice for her arm. When he returned, he held Callie tenderly, applying the ice and reassuring her. Paul took a deep breath, realizing he'd never seen the deep bond between them, how close and connected they were. Their battles were a sibling form of loving contact, separating while staying connected. His eyes filled with tears of relief; he knew his kids would be all right.

When we step out of time, we see each moment anew, just as it is, without preconceptions. Zen Master Shunryu Suzuki famously called this "beginner's mind." Suzuki Roshi repeated these simple, liberating teachings of living here and now to all who would listen, including a young Zen priest from Japan who had come to assist the San Francisco community. After some weeks, the new teacher complained that his English was too limited to communicate the essence of Zen to his students. The next day Suzuki Roshi went into the *zendo* (meditation hall) and took the teacher's seat. He rang the bell and put his hands together. With slow, careful words he said, "Today is today." *Long pause.* "Today is not yesterday." *Long pause.* "Today is not tomorrow." *Long pause.* "Today is today." Then he smiled, bowed, and left. "Five words," he later told the young teacher. "All you need to teach Zen."

One day at a time is how the twelve-step program puts it. Novelist Storm Jameson explains, "There is only one world, the world pressing against you at this minute. There is only one minute in which you are alive, this minute here and now. The only way to live is by accepting each minute as an unrepeatable miracle."

Freedom and the presence of love come alive in the here and now. Love in the past is a memory. Love in the future is a fantasy. The only place to truly love is just where you are.

How Then Shall We Live?

In a now-famous psychology experiment, researchers asked two separate groups of students to cross the Princeton University campus to attend what they were told was an important lecture on the parable of the Good Samaritan, the biblical model for stopping to help a stranger. The first group was told to hurry because the lecture doors would be closing soon. The second group of students was told that the lecture was going to start soon, but that they needn't rush and could go in whenever they got there. As individuals from each group crossed the campus, they passed someone who seemed to be injured and in need of help. No one in either group knew that the person who seemed to be in trouble was pretending to be injured.

Yet almost every student in the first group, having been told to hurry, passed right by the injured and needy person without stopping, even though they were on their way to hear a lecture about offering help to strangers. In contrast, most of the second group, those not in a hurry, saw the injured actor and kindly stopped to offer assistance. Hurry or care? Which way do you want to live?

Living in the present is the ground of liberation. But it is difficult; living in the present opens you to the full measure of life. It's easy to be here when life is pleasant, but what about when you experience pain, depression, hurt, anger, confusion, loneliness, or fear? Modern culture would tell you to distract yourself from the pain by going to a movie or shopping. Doctors prescribe tranquilizers so people grieving loss don't feel the pain. Our habits of distraction, hurriedness, and constantly making plans operate like addictions—they are a profound resistance to the present. To the extent that you distract yourself and bury yourself in busyness, you are not free.

Mindfulness and loving awareness are the antidotes, the gateways to freedom. When you recognize exactly what is present, even if it's pain, anxiety, anger, or grief, you can acknowledge it gently, as if bowing to it. As you do, you will feel love grow and the space of ever-present loving awareness, which can hold it all, now.

Finding Sanctuary

"*Now.* That's the key," says Pema Chödrön.

Now, now, now. Mindfulness trains you to be awake and alive, fully curious, about what? Well, about now, right? You sit in meditation and the breath is now, and waking up from your fantasies is now and even the fantasies are now, although they seem to take you into the past and the future. The more you can be completely now, the more you realize you're in the center of the world, standing in the middle of a sacred circle. It's no small affair, whether you're brushing your teeth or cooking your food or wiping your bottom. Whatever you are doing, you are doing it now!" (emphasis added)

The good thing is you can easily increase your capacity to live now through practicing mindfulness and loving awareness. Neuroscience shows that mindful awareness can measurably develop in just weeks of training. And with awareness grows resilience, greater access to compassion, neural integration, emotional stability, inner regulation, physical healing, and joy.

Mindfulness centers you here and now. Dr. Rachel Remen compares it to finding your *querencia*:

> *In bullfighting there is a place in the ring where the bull feels safe. If he can reach this place, he stops running and can gather his full strength. He is no longer afraid . . . It is the job of the matador to know where this sanctuary lies, to be sure the bull does not have time to occupy his place of wholeness. This safe place for the bull is called the* querencia. *For humans, the* querencia *is the safe place in our inner world. When a person finds their* querencia, *in full view of the matador, they are calm and peaceful. Wise. They have gathered their strength around them.*

As you practice mindfulness, you discover your *querencia*. Try it. Become centered, still. Step out of time. You can do this. Wherever you are, with loving awareness, you can meet the full measure of human life, and trust that your heart is big enough to open to it.

Timelessness of the Natural World

Nature can open the gates of heaven in a moment, whether we look closely at a flower or lift our eyes to the expanse of an open field. Step outdoors and visit with the plum trees, cumulus clouds, hummingbirds, evening winds, sunrise, or flowing water. Let go of thoughts and plans and rest in the timeless reality of the natural world. American sage Ralph Waldo Emerson explains, "The roses under my window make no reference to former roses or to better ones, they are what they are. There is no time to them. There is simply the rose. It is perfect in every moment of its existence."

In Bali, where I have lived, the culture is full of timeless offerings. Each day is marked by a round of ritual, music, prayer, and dance. Individuals take sacred pauses from their tasks regularly, from the shining morning to the night. There is little emphasis on reading few spiritual books. An elder there explained to me, "We don't read books, we read the stars." Looking at the night sky, seeing the great arc of the Milky Way, you come back to the ever-present mystery.

In the modern world, with its air-conditioning and cars, computers, and ultraclean hospitals, we have forgotten nature and mystery. Our powerful modern medicine, with its gifts of antibiotics, MRIs, and surgery, is missing some important things. As the healer and author Loren Slater writes:

> In this time of managed care, more emphasis seems to be placed upon medication and the quick amelioration of symptoms, short-term work and privatized, profit-making clinics, than upon the lovely and mysterious alchemy that comprises the healthy cords between and within people, the cords that soothe [our] terrors and help us heal.

Her words remind us of the blessings that come from tending life as it unfolds. Freedom is fulfilled not through distracted hurrying, but through living here and now. Mindfulness shows us that there is no other place to be. To live in the present does not deny our human capacity to care for our responsibilities. It's just knowing that everything happens now. Whatever we carry—our difficulties, problems, and cares—we meet them best by being present here and now. In this moment, we can acknowledge the tasks and concerns and then answer them with our heart.

Lover of the Moment

As you hold this book in your hands, take a deep breath. Let your mind quiet and your heart soften. You are here, in vastness and eternity. You can hold it all with wisdom. A Tibetan poet describes it this way:

> *One hand on the beauty of the world,*
> *One hand on the suffering of all beings,*
> *And two feet grounded in the present moment.*

A few years ago, at a Washington, DC, conference on compassion, a television crew interviewed the Dalai Lama. With the big cameras and lights pointed at him, the news anchor described the conference and noted that the Dalai Lama's book *The Art of Happiness* had spent many months on the *New York Times* bestseller list. Looking for a newsworthy angle, the anchor asked, "So, could you tell our viewers about one of the happiest times of your life?" The Dalai Lama paused and reflected, his eyes twinkling. Then he said, with a laugh, "I think now."

Living in the present unburdens you. Don't worry too much. You can envision and acknowledge your life's complexity but do so in the present, so you do not lose the vitality of life. French Nobel laureate André Gide confessed, "To be utterly happy, the only thing necessary is to refrain from comparing this moment with other moments." Look around. See the people, the scene, sense the warmth of your body, feel the mood and your pulsing heart. If you were in danger of losing your life, what wouldn't you give for a moment like this? Take a breath. Treasure it. Smile.

Become a lover of the moment. France, known for its leisurely meals, has resisted fast food and celebrates the slow food movement. To paraphrase the Pointer Sisters, "I want a lover with a slow hand and an easy touch"; you, too, can be a lover of the present. This doesn't mean that now can't include speed, confusion, ambition, running, creative competition, and joyful abandon. It can. *Now* includes it all.

To open your senses and your heart, however, it does help to slow down. One of the poets in my neighborhood, Barbara Ruth, explains, "I once walked the six miles from my house to Kent Lake in less than four hours, but that wasn't my best time. My personal best is eight hours and fifteen minutes. That includes time resting with a lizard sunning on the rocks; writing down a dream remembered starting at Mt. Barnabe; listening to a woodpecker knock herself against the tree that harbors the osprey's nest."

That's for You

Living here and now brings beauty and mystery. Watch how children play. They know they will be called home, yet they give themselves fully to their adventures. You, too, will be called, as we all will. But for now, why not live fully awake? Fully inhabiting the present, you can plant seeds for a future that will unfold in due season.

Anthropologist Gregory Bateson tells the story of one of Oxford University's oldest colleges:

The magnificent main hall there was built in the early 1600s with oak beams forty feet long and four feet thick. Recently they began to suffer from dry rot, and administrators couldn't find English oaks large enough to replace them. A young faculty member said, "Why don't we ask the college forester if some of the lands given to Oxford might have enough trees to call upon?" They brought in the forester, who said, "We've been wondering when you would ask. When the present hall was constructed three hundred and fifty years ago, the architects specified that a grove of trees be planted and maintained to replace the beams in the ceiling when they suffered from dry rot.

Bateson's comment was, "That's the way to run a culture."

Living now frees your heart to transform all you touch. As William Butler Yeats writes, when you are fully present "others live a clearer, perhaps even fiercer life because of it." Each moment of presence is an act of courage. Whether it brings you tears or joy, living in the present offers you a precious gift, the benevolence of being at home in this mysterious universe.

David Armitage tells how he had begun a rigorous six-year academic program in Boston that required him to work full-time during the day, take classes at night, and do homework on the weekends. He says, "On my first summer off, I wanted to get far away from my studies, work with my hands, and be close to the earth. So, I went to live with an Amish family in Pennsylvania. The experience renewed me, and I decided to do it again the next summer.

"That year I drove from Boston to Pennsylvania on a holiday weekend, and what was normally a six-hour trip took more than ten hours. By the time I arrived, just before dusk, I was anxious and exhausted.

"My Amish hosts had delayed their dinner for me. During the meal, I tried to act natural, but I felt full of nerves. My Amish host could clearly tell something was amiss, because at the end of dinner he said, 'Come with me.'

"I followed him to their backyard, which bordered an alfalfa field. Although his faith discouraged smoking, the farmer lit a cigarette. Three of his children gamboled about while two others clung to him. The farmer stood without saying a word, looking out over the alfalfa. I did the same.

"The dark-green field was becoming harder to see in the fading light. The sky was peach at the horizon and deep blue higher up. Stars had begun to appear. Then out of the alfalfa rose fireflies—a few at first, but soon there were hundreds. Their pinpricks of light mingled with the stars: heaven and earth meeting in this humble man's backyard. I felt my nervousness leave me.

"The farmer turned and said, 'That's for you.'"

The presence of eternity is right where you are. Each step, each word, each breath is an invitation. Give yourself the gift of silence, of listening. Go out into the woods, the mountains, walk along a meandering stream or the ever-changing sea. Look closely at a hundred kinds of steady, leafing trees. Follow the delicate flight of birds. Marvel at the strange gait of human bipeds. Listen for the laughter of children. When you are in difficulty, remember the world beckons to you with a bigger story. It invites you to vastness and freedom.

PRACTICE
Open to Timelessness

Let yourself be seated comfortably, with ease and presence. In this practice, you will sit in timeless loving awareness and let yourself become what Ajahn Chah called "the One Who Knows," the witness to all things.

Be dignified and relaxed, and sense yourself taking your seat at the still point of the turning world. Let experiences, sensations, thoughts, sounds, sights appear like water pouring from a fountain or images on a screen. Poignant memories, luminous sunsets, all your joys and pains are on endless creative display, appearing and dissolving.

It is always now, the eternal present. Even as a child playing outdoors, you knew how to step outside of time. See how time, clocks, calendars, future, past, plans, and memories are all ideas created by the mind. Shift your attention. Rest as timeless loving awareness, the One Who Knows. All that appears are simply motions in space that cannot affect the ground of eternity.

Sense vastness. Galaxies turn in the timeless universe, life renews itself again and again. It is not your body, but eternity's body, known by eternity's awareness.

It is always now. Breathe.

Rest in spacious silence. Trust.

And when you get up, let your actions arise out of stillness. Resting in eternity you will naturally know how to respond, create, embody. But the actions will arise from the One Who Knows. Lao Tzu, the Taoist sage, says, "Remain unmoving until the right action arises by itself."

Part Two

Obstacles to Freedom

*God, send us the cure. The sickness
we've got already.*

—TEVYE, IN *FIDDLER ON THE ROOF*

Chapter 5

Fear of Freedom

People often prefer a very limited,
punishing regime—rather than
face the anxiety of freedom.

—JEAN-PAUL SARTRE

A long with the joy of freedom is a fear of the unknown. Freedom can be *both* exhilarating and unnerving. The conflict runs deep. When a rabbit runs free, it has to watch for the hawk. Hunter-gatherers feared going too far afield, knowing they might encounter wild beasts or danger from other clans. Sergeant James Walker redeployed to Iraq four times, not only because of the camaraderie, intensity, aliveness, and a sense of belonging to something important, but because "it was harder to stay home and face all the confusing choices of civilian life."

Trauma, Fear, and Freedom

Fear of freedom can arise in many circumstances. Sometimes it is linked to unresolved trauma. In times of danger, accident, or conflict, our "fight, flight, or freeze" mechanism is activated. The human survival instinct is so strong that our body and mind shift to an automatic protective response. At the time of trauma, our conscious mind does not fully allow in the overwhelming experience. Instead, the trauma can get locked in and persist long after the event. Traumatic memories are held in the body, where they can trigger painful memories and fear of taking action or of loving. Trauma can be locked in with denial, addiction, and other patterns of avoidance. We become like the bear in a local zoo who paced her enclosure, back and forth, for fifteen years. When the zoo finally expanded the bear habitat, creating a spacious enclosure with a pond and trees, the poor bear continued to pace the same eighteen feet she had followed for years, back and forth.

Freeing yourself from trauma requires finding a source of inner stability from which you can approach the reservoir of pain and fear. This may be as simple as sensing some place in your body that feels calm, strong, and unaffected—the soles of your feet, your "sit" bones, your strong shoulders. Or it may come by invoking a memory of freedom and well-being in a special spot in nature, or feeling safe and loved with your grandparents or any other safe place you've been. Often in facing trauma, to avoid being overwhelmed, you also need the help and the presence of another. Then, when you find some ground of inner stability, and you have the support to gently approach the trauma, little by little you can feel its pain, listen to its story, and release the holding in the body. This gradual opening allows your traumatized nervous system to digest the past without being retraumatized and to arrive step by step to freedom.

Resolving trauma can take time, a repeated willingness to experience and process what is unfinished. Lloyd Burton, a Vietnam veteran who is now a Buddhist teacher, used mindfulness and lovingkindness to find healing from the war. In his own words, Lloyd describes a meditation retreat where he found redemption for the terrible atrocities he'd witnessed as a soldier.

I served as a field medical corpsman with the Marine Corps ground forces in the early days of the war, stationed in the mountainous provinces on the border of what was then North and South Vietnam. Our casualty rates were high, as were those of the villagers we treated when circumstances permitted.

After returning home, I had a recurring nightmare at least twice a week. I dreamed I was back in Vietnam facing the same dangers, witnessing the same incalculable suffering, and I'd wake up suddenly—alert, sweating, scared. This went on for eight years until I attended my first meditation retreat.

At the retreat, nightmares filled my mind's eye not just at night but during the day as well, at sittings, during walking meditations, and at meals. Horrific wartime flashbacks overlay the retreat center's quiet redwood grove. Sleepy students in the dorm became body parts strewn about a makeshift morgue on the DMZ. As I relived these memories, I endured for the first time the full emotional impact of experiences that thirteen years earlier, as a twenty-year-old medic, I was simply unprepared to withstand. My mind was bringing forth memories so terrifying, so life-denying, and so spiritually eroding that I didn't know I was still carrying them around. By openly facing what I feared most and had most strongly suppressed, a profound catharsis began to take place.

I had been plagued by the fear that if I allowed the inner demons of war to reach the surface, I would be consumed by them, but I experienced the opposite. The visions of slain friends and dismembered children slowly gave way to other half-remembered scenes: the entrancing, intense beauty of the jungle, a thousand different shades of green, a fragrant breeze blowing over beaches so white and dazzling they seemed carpeted by diamonds. What also arose was a deep sense of forgiveness for my past and present self: compassion for the idealistic, young, would-be healer and physician forced to witness the unspeakable obscenities of what humankind is capable and for the haunted veteran who had not let go of memories he couldn't even acknowledge he carried.

The compassion has stayed with me. And through practice and continued inner relaxation, it has grown to encompass those around me as well, when I'm free enough to allow it to do so. While the full range of memories have stayed with me, the nightmares have not.

The last of my sweating screams happened in silence, fully awake, at a retreat in Northern California many years ago.

You, too, can open to freedom after trauma through compassion.

Self-Hatred

The fear of freedom runs deep. Often it arises with a sense of unworthiness. Many years ago, I went with a group of Western meditation teachers to meet with the Dalai Lama. We asked for his advice dealing with the widespread self-hatred and frequent sense of unworthiness experienced by Western students. "Self-hatred?" the Dalai Lama asked, unable to grasp the concept. Apparently, this is so uncommon in Tibet that there is no word for it. He asked how many of the teachers themselves had experienced this. Most hands went up. A few minutes later, after a bewildered consulting with his translator to be sure he understood what we had told him, he looked at us with great sympathy. "But this is a mistake!" he exclaimed.

Unworthiness, self-hatred, shame, and guilt are a form of inner bondage. To judge yourself as inadequate or irredeemably blemished, to carry self-hatred is a form of inner torture, paralyzing your spirit. Even a modicum of unworthiness can stop you in your tracks. The release from this bondage, as veteran Lloyd Burton describes, begins with courage and love. You must develop compassion and tenderness toward your own life.

Practicing self-compassion is a wonderful way to heal

from shame, self-judgment, and self-hate. The ground of self-compassion is mindfulness, a clear, nonjudgmental awareness of whatever is present, including the self-judgment, shame, or self-hate. Awareness can begin by simply noticing how these states like unworthiness and shame feel in your body, the pain they carry, the anxiety, grief, fear, addiction, and other related emotions you feel, the stories they tell. You have so many ideas and ideals of how you should be that these cascade into unhealthy ways of judging yourself, instead of taking care of yourself, and loving who you actually are.

Next, you have to infuse this respectful presence of mindfulness with compassion and tenderness for all the pain and suffering you hold. Sometimes it can help to remember back to the first times you learned these painful patterns and thoughts, and imagine tenderly holding yourself as a child. Over and over you can evoke a respectful, tender holding of yourself with compassion. You can recite inwardly phrases such as "I treasure myself" and "I am worthy of love," or simply put your hand on your heart and imagine the compassionate touch you would get from Mother Teresa or the Dalai Lama.

As you feel this self-compassion, let yourself also reflect on your common humanity. You are only human. Like all humans, you will encounter pleasure and pain, praise and blame, difficulty and ease, success and failure, joy and sorrow. Remember that many other people in the world are experiencing the same struggles. It is who we are. With compassion and care we can build an empowered, healthy, loving life.

Trying to Please

Olivia was a well-known designer whose work life had become all-consuming. She was having trouble sleeping, and her relationships had frayed. She could hardly stop to connect with Fabien, her partner, and was often irritable with her teenage daughter, Joanna. She turned to mindfulness, but sitting quietly was difficult for her; she wanted to run away. Feeling stuck, she came to see me. A self-critical inner voice was demanding that she work more. And even though she knew this was a trap, she felt ashamed, uncertain, afraid her business would somehow fail, and guilty she wasn't there for Joanna and Fabien. As she held these feelings, fear arose. "I am so afraid of disappointing everyone, including myself," she said, and began to weep.

As we sat together, I asked when she first had felt this fear. Her eyes opened wide as she remembered, and she said, "When I was three." Her family had been despondent. Her dad was mostly on the road; her mom was miserable, self-centered, and drinking heavily. Olivia had tried to please her parents but got almost nothing back except irritability and occasional disapproval. Now at fifty-one, she realized she'd been looking to get approval for her actions her whole life.

"Hold this three-year-old Olivia in your gaze and your heart," I counseled. Her face softened immediately, and her eyes became moist. "I just wanted them to love me," she said, and she began to weep. "I thought there was something wrong and that it must be me. I still feel small and ashamed. How long I have tried to please everyone." Holding herself as if she were a child, Olivia learned to practice compassion for herself and to recognize the pain and self-judgment inside her. Slowly she began to let love in.

Over many weeks this process brought Olivia to review the whole of her work life and her family. She saw how her sense of being unworthy had driven her to success, and that in the process she had abandoned her tender feelings toward her daughter and her patient partner. Finally, she could let in how much they loved her, and almost instantly, she felt free to love them. She became almost giddy. "I can take them on a vacation. If I'm not feeling three years old, I can work more or not, grow my business, or even sell it. I can do whatever I choose when I don't feel so bad about myself."

What are your memories of trying to please? How have they shaped your life today? When you see the ways that you limit yourself, hold it all with tenderness and compassion, take a big breath, and realize you are free to find a new way to be.

Fear of Falling

Gandhi said, "Freedom is not worth having if it does not include the freedom to make mistakes." Don't be afraid of making mistakes. Step out. Fly. Even if you get burned, you can fall back to earth and start again. Zen Master Dogen laughingly called life "one continuous mistake." Yes, there is the fear of looking bad, but later when you review your life, will you wish you had held back? Probably not.

Sometimes, we limit our own freedom because we think it will overwhelm us. Or we think we don't deserve it. Or we fear that our ego will lead us astray, that we'll get too big for our britches and try to fly without restraint. We worry that if we act and express our true freedom, we will burn up or take a gigantic fall, as in the myth of Icarus. We constrain ourselves from being "too free."

Everyone stumbles. In the ordinary rhythm of life, we falter and then learn from our suffering. Sometimes we worry about our tendency to overreach, to dream up heady plans for ourselves, inflated visions of the future. Other times we feel inadequate or unworthy. Acknowledge these fears kindly. But don't follow their advice.

Carl felt confused and frozen every time he became focused and still in meditation. When we sat together, he became frightened. I asked him to be with this strong fear, to bring a kind attention to it, and to notice how it felt in his body. Then I invited him to let a key memory associated with the fear arise. An image arose of playing high school football really hard and accidentally breaking his opponent's arm, and he began to weep. Something in him was afraid he would hurt someone again. I suggested that he bring compassion to this fear of misusing his own power and causing pain to others. Carl obviously cared a lot about other people. Now he had to honor this care for others and for himself without letting it turn into fear.

Because modern life offers many possibilities, we may fear making a *wrong* choice. Listen to your heart, and consult your body and your head. Then, experiment, take a step, learn, discover, grow. You can enjoy even the mistakes; they are part of the game. All you can do is act with your best intentions, recognizing you cannot control the results.

Not knowing, a famous Zen practice, conveys the truth of life.

Acting freely, you cede control of the outcome and willingly cast your unique spirit into the mystery.

Acting Flawlessly

My friend Dr. Rachel Remen, author of the bestselling *Kitchen Table Wisdom*, tells a story about David, a resident physician at the large AIDS ward at San Francisco General Hospital in the early 1980s. It was during the AIDS epidemic, before protease inhibitors and other drug therapies became available, and almost all the patients with the disease died. Many of David's patients were young men close to his own age, people whose lives mattered deeply to him. He had hoped that his medical training would give him the skills to heal his patients. Through much of his residency, he felt overwhelmed by a sense of futility.

David happens to be a Buddhist, and it has always been his practice to pray for his patients. Even now, when a patient dies, he lights a candle on his altar at home and keeps it burning for forty-nine days. The whole time he was at San Francisco General, he prayed for each dying young man and lit a candle on his altar for him. Years later, he reflected that perhaps the reason he had been there wasn't to cure or rescue his patients. Perhaps he had been there so that no one died without having someone to pray for him. Perhaps, David realized, he had served his patients flawlessly.

William McFee writes, "If fate means for you to lose, give him a good fight anyhow." Don't worry when freedom seems daunting. In the Bible, angels of light always approach with the words

"Fear not." German Zen master and psychotherapist Karlfried Durckheim explains:

> *The person who, being really on the Way, falls upon hard times in the world, will not, as a consequence, turn to that friend who offers him refuge and comfort and encourages their old self to survive. Rather, he will seek out someone who will faithfully and inexorably help him to risk himself, so that he may endure the difficulty and pass courageously through it. Only to the extent that a person exposes himself over and over again to annihilation, can that which is indestructible be found within. In this daring lie dignity and the spirit of awakening.*

Philosopher Bertrand Russell goes further: "One should respect public opinion insofar as is necessary to avoid starvation and keep out of prison, but anything that goes beyond this is voluntary submission to an unnecessary tyranny." Martha Graham amplifies, "No artist is ahead of his time. He *is* his time."

No one has lived your life before. It is an adventure worth taking.

Lean into the Wind

Whether you are down on your luck or successful, the same basic fears and dangers can rise up. No one is exempt.

A few years ago, I was invited to teach the art of mindfulness and compassion to the entire student body at the Stanford Graduate School of Business. I had been briefed that many of the students, although highly accomplished, were so busy and driven academically, all the while making plans to enter high levels of corporate life, that they were losing touch with themselves, their friends and family, and what matters most in human life. I joked to the professor and the dean, "It sounds like they need soul retrieval," and they laughingly agreed. I brought a team of top CEOs and business leaders with me, friends who had coped with and navigated enormous stress using mindfulness and lovingkindness practices. Together we led the whole school through compassion practices and stories.

"I am inspired by all we have learned here," one student said, "but let me ask bluntly, are you saying that if I get to your level and make a ton of money, I still might not be happy?" The innocence and sincerity of the question—and the revelation it was for him—made us all laugh. Then we helped the students envision a wise life balanced with work, creativity, love, and a sense of the sacred. We noted that envisioning was only the start. They would need to continue to value what they had seen. They would need to find practices and make choices that create a healthy life. They would not be able to control the economy, but *this* form of success was in their own hands.

Follow your heart's values and don't be reluctant to lean into the wind. Whether you are in the middle of a divorce, a business disaster, loss, death, or on the verge of a huge success, make something good come of it. Our lives are unpredictable, but we always have choices. We are free to respond, moment by moment. Even though you may be anxious, fear is often excitement holding its breath. Let yourself sense life's vitality, know life's joyful and painful evanescence, and respond with your whole spirit.

As Zorba the Greek reminds us, "Life is trouble. Only death is not. To be alive is to undo your belt and look for trouble." Freedom offers a chance to live fully every day, true to our own spirit and gifts. Don't be afraid of praise or blame. And whether it is outer freedom, inner freedom, or both—they do come together—know that you can choose to be joyful.

In our busy, overly connected society, our attention is pulled in a thousand directions. Every day we get the whole world's news with our morning coffee and smartphone. Scientists estimate that there is more information in one day's *New York Times* than the average sixteenth-century person would hear in a lifetime. It is easy to feel overwhelmed by our electronic tethers that call on us to tweet, post, text, and email at all hours.

Take a breath. Pause. When your life feels too full, being reminded that you are free can be unsettling. It's okay. Yes, you are free to choose your attitude today—to be grateful, courageous, fearful, bitter, or loving. But more than that, you are free—with all the resultant consequences—to quit your job, start a business, get married or divorced, make a work of art, take in a foster child, travel to a new place, cancel your email account.

Freedom can be absolutely vertiginous. Fortunately, you don't have to make all these moves at once, or ever. In fact, you have already made the choices you are following. But you *are* free to change course. Your life is both constrained and free, with limitations and consequences. Follow the law or end up in prison. Drive on the correct side of the road or end up in the hospital or dead. The best way to handle the vastness of freedom is to quiet your mind and listen to your heart. Your heart will provide the loving, considered guidance to make the best choices, with the deepest, most honest understanding.

Elija, a young man who had been in jail and prison since the age of thirteen, explained his own challenge: "When I was twenty-one, I was released on parole. I stood on the street corner as the light turned from red to green and cycled back to red again. I just kept standing there. Then I realized I was waiting for someone to tell me when I could cross the street. All my years locked up had robbed me of my sense of inner freedom. That's when I began the mindfulness program. I had to get it back."

You can get your freedom back, too. Simplify. Turn off your devices and turn on Mozart. Prune your schedule, walk in nature, make fewer commitments. You can envision and create a life with more voluntary simplicity. Inwardly, your feeling of being overwhelmed is increased by worries and imagination. The vision of your self as separate brings fear. But you are part of the web of life, so you don't need to hold on so tightly. Ultimately, you are awareness itself. Zen Master Philip Kapleau assured his students that when their boundaries began to dissolve during retreats, "You can't fall out of the universe."

PRACTICE

Entering Difficulties with an Open Mind and an Open Heart

Here is a practice to help you step out of fear and difficulty, to discover that you also carry the wisdom beyond fear in yourself. It shows how your capacity to visualize and listen deeply can transform your heart.

Sit in a way that is comfortable. Allow your breath to settle and return to the present moment. Rest quietly for a time.

Now, picture an ongoing difficulty in your life that involves one or more other people.

Let yourself remember what it is like when you are in the midst of this difficulty. With your mind's eye, see as many details as you can. Where are you? Who are you with? Are you standing, sitting? Speaking, acting?

Now, become aware of how you feel in this situation. Notice the emotions and states of mind that you're experiencing. Notice, too, your level of bodily tension or discomfort and observe how you usually react in this situation.

Now, notice what everyone else is doing or saying in this difficult situation. Because this is only a visualization, you are completely safe, so although you may have experienced it as painful or frightening, you are safe to imagine being in the situation.

Become mindful of any strong feelings that are present, and name them to yourself gently, "fear, fear," "hurt, hurt," "frustration, frustration." With great kindness notice the vulnerability underneath all these strong feelings. Name whatever feeling arises and allow it to be held in loving awareness. We are all tender beings and we are all courageous beings.

Now, in the midst of this difficulty, if you are indoors, you hear a knock on the door. If you are outside, notice that a figure is walking toward you. Turn to whomever you are with in this situation and say, "Excuse me for a moment."

When you answer the door or turn back to the approaching figure, you will discover that a luminous being has come to visit you. Let yourself be surprised to see who has come: He or she is a figure of great compassion, understanding, and courage. It might be Buddha or Kwan Yin, it might be Mother Mary or Jesus, Solomon or Gandhi, or a wise grandparent—a being who most represents compassion and wisdom. See who appears.

Now imagine that this luminous figure greets you and asks, "Are you having a hard time?" Feel the warmth and care in their smile. "Let me help you. I'll show you how I would handle this. Give your body to me, and I will enter it and look like you, and you can become invisible and follow along. No one will notice that I have entered your body."

Now follow them back into the place of difficulty. Notice how their body feels as they enter. What states of mind and heart do they bring to this difficulty? Notice how they listen and respond. Visualize or imagine how this luminous being brings wisdom and compassion to your difficult circumstances. Let them show you for a time.

When they have completed what they can do, let them once again excuse themselves, and follow them back to where you met.

Here they give you back your body and resume their original form. Before they go, they offer you a gift. They reach into their robe and bring out a present for you, a clear symbol of exactly what you need to help in this difficulty. If you have trouble understanding the symbol or it is not clear, hold it up to the light. Allow yourself to see what it is. You can know.

Finally, this luminous being touches you gently and whispers into your ear a few words of advice. Let yourself hear or imagine or think of his or her words.

After you receive the advice and the gift, thank the figure who has helped you and allow them to leave. Open your eyes and return to the present.

It is an amazing discovery to know that these luminous and wise beings can appear in any moment. Their wisdom and courage are always available! Wisdom and courage are your birthright. They have been in you all along. They are in you now.

Now spend a moment reflecting on how they approached your difficulty and what you learned from them. What spirit did they bring to it? How did they listen, respond? Write down the words of wisdom they have offered and what you understand about the gift they have given to you.

As you reflect, remember how your body felt when you first entered your difficulty. Was there tension, rigidity, fear, upset, confusion? Now recall how this wisdom figure's body felt as they entered the difficulty. The wisdom figures bring with them a sense of physical relaxation, centeredness, graciousness. It is as if you already know what it feels like to bring graciousness and open-mindedness, courage, and wisdom to your most difficult struggles.

When you take time to quiet your mind and listen deeply, the solutions you need are revealed. The wisdom you seek is within you.

Chapter 6

Forgiveness

You wanna fly, you got to give up the shit
that weighs you down.

—TONI MORRISON, *SONG OF SOLOMON*

Disappointment, betrayal, and broken trust happen to everyone. You are neither the first nor the last to experience this. Betrayal is part of the human drama; you are in the company of millions in your anguish. When it happens, it hurts. Emotional pain registers in the same areas of the brain as physical pain. But the betrayal, loss, heartbreak, regret, and anxiety, the outrage, emptiness, heaviness, and sorrows that come with that pain are not the end of the story. They are a hard chapter. Feeling the universality of this struggle brings some ease and perspective. It's not only *your* pain. It is one of the pains of the human experience, and it requires your deepest wisdom and compassion to heal. And it requires that you learn to forgive.

Forgiving Yourself and Another

When my marriage of nearly thirty years ended, I felt shocked and at sea. Liana had been the love of my life, and I had imagined we'd be married until the end of our lives. But in the decade after our beloved daughter went off to college, I began to travel more, and my wife told me she wanted more time for her painting and herself. Our needs diverged, and even when we were together, it was clear we weren't making each other happy. I was under the delusion that if I tried harder to make her happy (not a wise strategy), I would become happier myself. In the end, we decided the best thing was to separate.

This was the beginning of a long inner process. I found myself repeatedly reviewing the whole thirty years. I wanted to understand what had been good and where I had gone wrong. Sometimes looking back felt obsessive, sometimes confusing, sometimes infuriating. It took all of my training in mindfulness and compassion to weather those painful years, and it demanded forgiveness of myself for my mistakes and expectations and projections. Equally it demanded a forgiveness of my ex-wife. It took deep, repeated practice, for as I forgave one thing of myself or her, another memory or difficulty would arise, and I would breathe and go into the pain and finally say, "This, too."

While the profound process of review and feeling each loss was critical and I had to willingly honor the particulars of our marriage and its end, that was not enough. Feeling distraught was still easily triggered; it felt like a never-ending cycle. What forgiveness

98

was asking of me was bigger and wiser. I had to hold the whole human dance, all marriages and divorces and especially my own, all human forms of love with their idealism and pain, their elevation and failure, their tenderness and brokenheartedness with forgiveness. For myself, for my ex-wife, for everyone we had known and shared our lives with and loved. I had to let it all be okay and realize that this does not define me. "How could a teacher of mindfulness and lovingkindness be getting divorced?" I was asked.

Like a human being, that's how.

Outwardly, as our life unfolds, we take on a multitude of identities and roles. As Shakespeare describes, "One man in his lifetime plays many parts," as we "strut and fret our hour upon the stage." We are taught to play the roles given us year by year— child and student, employee and lover, parent and professional, patient and healer. But these roles are not our true identities. And we can learn to see beyond them.

Your Spirit Is Not Bound by Your History

Ram Dass, a well-known teacher of Hindu practice, was born Jewish. A student at one of his classes asked if he had rejected Judaism. Ram Dass answered that he had great respect for Jewish teaching, especially appreciating the mystical traditions of Hassidism and Kabbala. "But remember," he quipped, "I'm only Jewish on my parents' side!"

Our family history does not define us. Sujatha Baliga, a former public defender, is now the director of the restorative-justice project at the National Council on Crime & Delinquency in Oakland. She was born and raised in Shippensburg, Pennsylvania, the youngest child of Indian immigrants. From as far back as she can remember, Sujatha was sexually abused by her father. In her early teens, she started dying her hair blue and cutting herself. Then at age fourteen, two years before her father died of a heart attack, she realized the cause of her misery: what her father had been doing was terribly wrong.

Despite the torments of her childhood, Sujatha excelled in school. As an undergraduate at Harvard, she decided that she wanted to become a prosecutor and lock up child molesters. After college, she moved to New York and worked with battered women while waiting to hear if she had been accepted to law school. When her boyfriend won a fellowship to start a school in Mumbai, she decided to follow him before beginning her first year of law school.

While in India, Sujatha had what she calls "a total breakdown." She remembers thinking, "Oh, my God, I've got to fix myself before I start law school." So, she decided to take a train to Dharamsala, the Himalayan city that is home to a large Tibetan exile community. There she heard Tibetans recount "horrific stories of losing their loved ones as they were trying to escape the invading Chinese Army," she told me. "Women getting raped, children made to kill their parents—unbelievably awful stuff. And I would ask them, 'How are you even standing, let alone smiling?' And everybody would say, 'Forgiveness.' And they're like, 'What are you so angry about?' And I told them, and they'd say, 'That's actually pretty crazy.'"

The family who operated the guesthouse where Sujatha was staying told her that people often wrote to the Dalai Lama for advice and suggested she try it. Sujatha wrote something like, "Anger is killing me, but it motivates my work. How do you work on behalf of oppressed and abused people without anger as the motivating force?" She dropped off the letter at a booth by the front gate of the Dalai Lama's compound and was told to come back in a week. When she did, instead of getting a letter in response, Sujatha was invited to meet with the Dalai Lama privately for an hour.

When they met, he gave her two pieces of advice. The first was to meditate. She said she could do that. The second, she says, was "to align myself with my enemy, to consider opening my heart to them. I laughed out loud. I'm like: 'I'm going to law school to lock those guys up! I'm not aligning myself with anybody.' He patted me on the knee and said, 'Okay, just meditate.'"

Sujatha Baliga returned to the United States and signed up for an intensive ten-day meditation course. At first, she had to learn to bring mindfulness to all her torment and pain. Then, as Sujatha learned the formal practice of lovingkindness, in which we bring compassion to ourselves, to our loved ones, to strangers, and then to people who have harmed us, her heart cracked. On the final day of the course, she had a spontaneous experience of forgiveness of her father. She wept and somehow lost her desire for revenge and found the courage to continue her work out of compassion instead of rage. Last winter, sitting cross-legged on an easy chair in her home in Berkeley, she described the experience as a "relinquishment of anger, hatred, and the desire for retribution and revenge."

After graduating from law school, Sujatha clerked for a federal judge in Vermont. "That's when I first saw restorative justice in action," she says. Now a leader in the field, Sujatha carefully and slowly brings together perpetrators and victims who are willing to meet, in a delicate, painful process of listening, responding, understanding, forgiveness, and atonement. It is sacred work—the healing and redemption of broken souls. In this way, she fulfilled the second part of the Dalai Lama's prescription as well as the first.

You, too, can be released from the suffering of your history. While it is important to honor your past, it need not define you. Your identity is not limited to personal biography or your mind's ideas about itself. The stories we tell of our past are written on water. Research shows that much of what we remember isn't true. Even though it feels like an accurate recounting, it is cobbled together from associations, repeated stories, and imagination.

You are timeless. Whenever you forget this and identify with your mind's stories about who you are, look again.

Honoring the Past

In a famous story of ancient India, a young woman named Kisa Gotami had longed for years to have a child. After she finally gave birth, her infant son became sick and died, and she went mad from grief. Wandering dazed and carrying the body of her child, Kisa Gotami met an old man who heard her wails and told her to go see the Buddha. She begged the Buddha to bring her boy back to life, and, amazingly, he agreed. But first, he told her, she must bring him mustard seed, a common spice, from a family where no one had died. She went into the village and desperately went from compound to compound. They all had mustard seed to offer the weeping mother, but when she asked further, there was not one family who had not suffered the death of a brother, a daughter, an uncle, or a mother. Weary and tearful, Kisa Gotami began to realize that no family is exempt from the pain of mortality. She returned to the Buddha, still grieving but wiser now. He comforted her with compassion and gave her teachings of liberation that freed her heart even as she honored the death of her son.

Our culture still denies the reality of aging and death, or even birth. It was not long ago that pregnant single women were sent to homes for unwed mothers, shamed and hidden away for months. When their babies were due, they were taken to the hospital to give birth, their labor induced to fit the schedule of disapproving doctors, and then their babies were taken away. The women were then sent back to their homes with the instruction "You are not to talk about this to anyone!" Imagine giving birth, one of the most powerful of all human experiences, then being forbidden to speak of it, to pretend this life-changing event hadn't happened.

To be free from the past, you must recognize what happened and feel its hold on you. It is here, consciously or unconsciously, held in your body, feelings, and mind. It is critical to honor the loss before you can take the next step of letting go. Then you can practice forgiveness and with it use meditation, therapy, trauma work, art, and intimate support to help touch and heal the betrayal and trauma.

Heart of Forgiveness

To forgive and be free, you must honor your measure of grief, betrayal, the whole difficult story, and hold it with all the compassion you can. Remember that you are bigger than anything that happens to you. Then you can turn your heart toward forgiveness.

Molly, an economics graduate of a top school, was manager of a nonprofit supporting homeless women. When she came to see me, she was so exhausted and overwhelmed, and she was working only part-time. Depression and anxiety were her default states, and she was extremely sensitive to slights. It was easy to understand as she carried a deep grief. Her parents had been drinking and absent for most of her lonely childhood; when they were present, they were cruel and judgmental. Even as an adult, as she labored to make her way successfully through college and her career, she rarely felt joy or ease.

To free herself, Molly took up the practice of compassion. She took her burden of loneliness and sadness to Quan Yin, the Chinese goddess of compassion, as many turn to Mother Mary. She practiced this way for months and felt held by a tenderness without judgment. Eventually, by the end of the year, she envisioned her cruel parents in Quan Yin's lap.

One afternoon, as her heart grew easier, she reflected on the neglect and impoverishment of her past and saw that defining herself by her abusive upbringing had begun to dissolve. Not that the suffering hadn't happened, but it was long over and she could let it go. As the sun shone on the blue oriental carpet in her living room and dazzled the yellow pansies in the window box, she realized this was the first moment in her life she felt consciously happy.

Courage and Clarity

Forgiving ourselves and others is the ground for healing. Without it, our lives are chained, and we are forced to repeat the suffering of the past without release. Consider this dialogue between two former prisoners of war:

"Have you forgiven your captors yet?"

"No, never!"

"Well, then, they still have you in prison, don't they?"

Without forgiveness, we perpetuate the illusion that hatred can heal our pain and the pain of others. Even people who have suffered in the tragic wars and conflicts of Bosnia, Cambodia, Rwanda, Northern Ireland, and South Africa have had to find pathways to forgiveness. Sometimes this requires forgiving the unforgivable, consciously releasing the heart from the clutches of another's terrible acts. No matter what traumas our past holds, we must discover ways to move on. It's the only way to heal.

Forgiveness requires courage and clarity. People mistakenly believe the process is to forgive and forget. Forgiveness does not forget, nor does it condone the past. It acknowledges what is unjust, harmful, and wrong. It bravely recognizes the suffering of the past and understands the conditions that brought it about. With forgiveness, you can also say, "Never again will I allow these things to happen. Never again will I permit such harm to come to myself or others."

Forgiveness does not mean you must continue to be in touch with those who have harmed you. In some cases, the best practice may be to sever your connection, once and for all. Sometimes in the process of forgiveness, a person who hurt or betrayed you may wish to make amends, but even that doesn't require you to put yourself in the way of further harm. In the end, forgiveness simply means never putting another person out of your heart.

The practice of forgiveness takes time. It does not simply paper over what happened. Nor does it ask you to suppress or ignore pain. Coming to forgiveness may include a lengthy process of grief, outrage, sadness, loss, and pain. It is a deep unfolding that honors the grief and hurt over and over in the heart. And in its own time, forgiveness ripens into the freedom to truly let go.

Most important, we must forgive ourselves for any harm we have caused. Just as others have been caught in suffering, so have we. Awakening forgiveness for ourselves is essential. If we look honestly at our lives, we can see the sorrows and pain that have led to our own bad acts. Holding the pain we have caused with compassion, we can extend forgiveness to ourselves. Without mercy for ourselves, we will always live in exile. As author Maxine Hong

Kingston, who has led a war veterans' writing group for twenty years, says, the group's motto is, "Tell the truth, and so make peace."

True Release

The book *Offerings at the Wall* is a photographic collection of letters and offerings that have been placed at the Vietnam Veterans Memorial in Washington, DC. It visibly conveys the power of forgiveness. I have regularly visited that long black stone wall with 58,000 names, and I have seen many stand there in silence, some leaving flowers, some only tears. One of the images in the book is a small, hand-tinted reproduction of a photograph of a Vietnamese soldier and a little girl that was left there by an American vet in 1989 with this note:

Dear Sir,

For twenty-two years I have carried your picture in my wallet. I was only eighteen years old that day we faced one another on that trail in Chu Lau, Vietnam. Why you did not take my life I'll never know . . . Forgive me for taking your life, I was reacting just the way I was trained . . . So many times over the years I've stared at your picture and your daughter. Each time my heart and guts would burn with the pain of guilt. I have two daughters of my own now. I perceive you as a brave soldier, defending his homeland.

Above all else I can now respect the importance life held for you. I suppose that is why I am able to be here today. It is time for me to continue the life process and release the pain and guilt. Forgive me, sir.

Richard Luttrell, the soldier who wrote this letter, lived with remorse and soul-searching for many years. Eventually he flew back to Vietnam to try to return this photograph and ask forgiveness. In Hanoi, the authorities directed him to a rural village. There he found the now-grown daughter and son of the man he had killed. He explained who he was and wept as he handed them a copy of the picture. They joined him in tears. He asked their forgiveness. They were touched that he had come. Later they told him that they could feel their father's loving spirit had now been born in him.

No matter how extreme the circumstances, a release from the past is possible. Confronting violence and abuse, that of others or our own, often requires a powerful response. And then we also practice forgiveness, so a fuller freedom can be born.

I'm Going to Kill You

On a train from Washington to Philadelphia, I was seated next to Robert Brown, an African American who had worked for the US State Department in India and quit to run a rehabilitation program for juvenile offenders in the District of Columbia. Most of the youths he worked with were gang members who had committed homicide. One fourteen-year-old boy in the program, who had been living on the street before the killing, had shot and killed an innocent teenage boy to prove himself to his gang. At the trial, the victim's mother sat impassive, silent until the end, when the youth was convicted of the murder. After the verdict was announced, she stood up slowly and stared directly at the boy and stated, "I am going to kill you." Then the young man was taken away to serve several years in the juvenile facility.

After the first year, the mother of the slain child went to visit his killer. He'd had no other visitors to the facility. For a time, they talked, and when she left, she gave him some money for cigarettes. Then, gradually, she started to visit him more regularly, bringing food and small gifts. Near the end of his three-year sentence, she asked him what he would be doing when he got out. He was uncertain, so she offered to set him up with a job at a friend's company. Then she inquired where he would live, and since he had no family to return to, she offered him temporary use of the spare room in her home.

For eight months, he lived there, ate her food, and worked at the job. Then one evening she called him into the living room to talk. She sat across from him and waited. Then she started. "Do you remember in the courtroom when I said I was going to kill you?"

"I sure do," he replied.

"I did not want a boy who could kill my son for no reason to remain alive on this earth. I wanted him to die. That's why I started to visit you and bring you things. That's why I got you the job and let you live here in my house. That's how I set about changing you. And that old boy, he's gone. Now I want to ask you, since my son is gone and that killer is gone, if you'll stay here. I've got room and I'd like to adopt you if you'll let me." And she became the mother of her son's killer, the mother he never had.

Letting Go: The Chord That Completes the Song

Ajahn Chah taught me, "If you let go a little, you have a little peace. If you let go a lot, you have a lot of peace. If you let go completely, you are truly free." Letting go is key. But the term *letting go* can be confusing. We think it means to push away the past, but that is not correct. Rejecting and resisting, we stay connected, tied in a struggle. "Letting *be*" might express the freedom of release more accurately. There is a felt sense, an intuition in you that knows when you have released the holding in your heart. It's like the chord that completes a song.

To come to this level of resolution, you need to honor the depth of your difficulties with mindfulness and care. As you make friends with your past, as you bring compassion to it, gradually the past will lose its power. Over time, the pains of your childhood, the struggles and traumas of past years, become workable, a little softer and a little less toxic. Though you acknowledge the scars you carry in your body and memory, they need not define you. You can shift your focus instead to your well-being. You might say, I acknowledge the difficulty, but I will not let it overwhelm my heart. Zen teacher Ed Brown expresses this in a *gatha,* a mindfulness poem:

Washing my hands
I cleanse my mind
of the same old thinking . . .
and offer to lend a hand
to each new task.

Moving on means letting go of thoughts that obsess about the past, letting go of betrayal, conflict, and disappointment. Through forgiveness for ourselves and others, we let it be past. We move on with the current of our life, acknowledging what has happened without being limited by it.

PRACTICE

Forgiveness Meditation

To practice forgiveness meditation, let yourself sit comfortably. Allow your eyes to close and your breath to be natural and easy. Let your body and mind relax. Breathing gently into the area of your heart, let yourself feel all the barriers you have erected and the emotions that you have carried because you have not forgiven—not forgiven yourself, not forgiven others. Let yourself feel the pain of keeping your heart closed. Then, breathing softly, begin asking and extending forgiveness, reciting the following words, letting the images and feelings that come up grow deeper as you repeat them.

ASKING FORGIVENESS OF OTHERS

Recite and reflect: *"There are many ways that I have hurt and harmed others, have betrayed or abandoned them, caused them suffering, knowingly or unknowingly, out of my pain, fear, anger, and confusion."* Let yourself remember and visualize the ways you have hurt others. See and feel the pain you have caused out of your own fear and confusion. Become aware of your own sorrow and feel your regret. Sense that finally you can release this burden and ask for forgiveness. Picture one or more memory that still burdens your heart. And then, one at a time, to each person in your mind repeat: *"In the ways I have hurt you out of my fear, pain, anger, and confusion, I ask your forgiveness, I ask your forgiveness. May I be forgiven."*

OFFERING FORGIVENESS TO YOURSELF

Recite: *"Just as I have harmed others, there are many ways that I have hurt and harmed myself. I have betrayed or abandoned myself many times in thought, word, or deed, knowingly and unknowingly."* Feel your own precious body and life. Let yourself see the ways you have hurt or harmed yourself. Picture them, remember them. Feel the sorrow you have carried from this and sense that you can release these burdens. Extend forgiveness for each of them, one by one. Repeat to yourself: *"For the ways I have hurt myself through action or inaction, out of fear, pain, and confusion, I now extend a full and heartfelt forgiveness. I forgive myself, I forgive myself."*

OFFERING FORGIVENESS TO THOSE WHO HAVE HURT OR HARMED YOU

Recite and reflect: *"There are many ways that I have been harmed by others, betrayed, abused, or abandoned, knowingly or unknowingly, in thought, word, or deed."* Let yourself picture and remember these many ways. Feel the sorrow you have carried from this past and sense that you can release this burden of pain by extending forgiveness whenever your heart is ready. Now say to yourself: *"I now remember the one or many of the ways others have hurt or harmed me, wounded me, out of their fear, pain, confusion, and anger. I have carried this pain in my heart too long. To the extent that I am ready, I offer you forgiveness. To those who have caused me harm, I offer my forgiveness, I forgive you."*

Let yourself gently repeat these three directions for forgiveness until you feel a release in your heart. For some great pains, you may not feel a release but only the burden and the anguish or anger you have held. Touch this softly. Be forgiving of yourself for not being ready to let go and move on. Forgiveness cannot be forced; it cannot be artificial. You can simply set the intention to forgive, continuing to practice and let the words and images work gradually in their own way. In time, you can make the forgiveness meditation a regular part of your life, letting go of the past and opening your heart to each new moment with a wise lovingkindness.

Chapter 7

Freedom from Troubled Emotions

Give me everything mangled and bruised,
and I will make a light of it to make you weep,
and we will have rain and we will begin again.

—DEENA METZGER

Freedom does not mean fighting against or suppressing troubled emotions. That would be another form of tyranny. To be free, you first need to be conscious of them and then you can learn to work with them wisely.

Praying for Our Enemies

Several years ago, I helped coordinate a meeting about prison reform and human transformation, bringing together the Dalai

Lama and twenty-five former convicts, all recently released from US prisons. Most had done long years in state penitentiaries and were invited because they had been changed by joining one of the Prison Dharma Network mindfulness programs offered by volunteers around the country.

The Dalai Lama brought two young Tibetan nuns, part of the Drapchi 14 who had been imprisoned as teenagers for reciting prayers in Tibet in public. The American prisoners spoke first, telling their stories of suffering and transformation, informing the Dalai Lama about the benefits of wisdom-training programs and offering eye-opening details about the horrendous, overcrowded cruelty of American prisons, the largest prison system in the world.

They told stories of inner struggle and the years they'd worked courageously to transform their lives. One of the former prisoners, Anita, was a thirty-nine-year-old woman whose warmth was immediately apparent. She'd been released two years earlier after serving fourteen years as a reluctant accomplice to a botched armed robbery. Anita described how hardened and territorial she and the women around her became in the degrading conditions of prisons. To stay sane sharing their tiny, high-security cells, the women established simple routines and strict boundaries. Periodically their routines would be disrupted by the intrusion of short-timers, women serving less than a year, who because of overcrowding were forced to double up in long-term cells. The short-termers were usually pushed away and ignored.

When Noni, a quiet woman, came into Anita's cell for four

months, Anita was wary of her. "This is where you can put your things, here's the part of the cell you use, and don't go beyond it," she told her new cellmate. For many days, Anita observed as her new cellmate sat sick and depressed on her bed and would hardly take food. Then she began to throw up, especially in the mornings. Finally, it dawned on Anita that Noni was pregnant.

Anita thought about this young woman and the baby. It didn't seem right for this depressed young mother-to-be to starve herself. She was hurting her baby. Anita found herself comforting Noni and listening to the story of her life. Slowly, she became her confidante, her protector, her supporter, making her more comfortable and making sure she was eating. Word about the pregnant girl got out, and women up and down the maximum-security cellblock began to help with special food and comfort. The compassion for Noni and her baby became communal; it brought the prisoners together.

Some months after Noni was released, news came back that her child, named Julia, had been safely delivered. The prisoners, who felt themselves to be Julia's aunties and grandmothers, cheered. New life had touched the sorrow of their cells. More than anyone, Anita was changed. The new life in Noni had opened Anita's barricaded heart and started her on a six-year path of healing and redemption. Anita, who had felt so hard and closed off from others, discovered new life in herself. Now Anita works full-time on projects that bring hope to incarcerated women.

After the American prisoners spoke about the trials of their years inside, the Dalai Lama invited the two young nuns to talk.

They described living through years of being beaten, starved, tortured with electric prods, and how through it all, they kept reciting their prayers. The Dalai Lama asked them if they had ever been afraid. They said yes. Their greatest fear was that they would lose compassion and allow hatred in their hearts. There was only one thing we could do, they said. "We prayed for the enemy." Then one of the burly, tattooed ex-cons from Louisiana spoke with moist eyes: "I've seen bravery in prison, but nothing like you girls."

These stories, whether descriptions of extreme circumstances or of common difficulties, remind us what is possible this very day. Amid your own joy and trouble, how is your spirit today? Are you caught, defeated, sad? Have you lost faith? Like Elija, who had been in prison since becoming a teenager, are you in some way stuck waiting for the light and the circumstances to change? You can step out. Whether you're at work, in your family or community, or just within your own body, your spirit is free. It's important to remember this when we're face-to-face with trauma.

Powerful Inner Forces

Modern psychology catalogs three hundred mental disorders. Psychoanalysis speaks of the primitive id. Neuroscience describes a reptilian brain below every human cortex. Spiritual traditions have lists of deadly sins, destructive emotions, inner demons, temptations, and poisons of the mind. We all recognize how the human mind can be taken over by greed, lust, rage, pride, jealousy, envy, delusion, hate, miserliness. These powerful forces sweep through people, across communities and nations.

The first step in working with these difficult energies is to see them clearly. Use the power of mindfulness, of loving awareness. Chloe, a young woman who came to a teen retreat, recounted that she had often gotten lost in depression, drinking, cutting herself, and other self-destructive behaviors. She had rejected every suggestion offered by her parents, but one desperate afternoon, she picked up a book in her mother's library on mindfulness and yoga. "It was like finding an amazing, powerful medicine in my hands, almost too good to be true. It showed me I could be aware of my thoughts and feelings but not have to believe them!" she said. By mindfully acknowledging her feelings, Chloe found that she didn't feel so stuck, and things began to change.

Loving awareness allows us to step outside the praise-and-blame paradigm. When we are unconscious, caught in states like judgment, anger, rigidity, compulsion, and prejudice, we blindly act out these feelings. And then we blame these problems on others. Yet if we look more deeply at them, we discover that our own insecurity and vulnerability often underlie the blame. We blame because we find these states hard to tolerate. James Baldwin writes, "One of the reasons people cling to their hate and prejudice so stubbornly is that they sense once hate is gone, they will be forced to deal with their own pain."

When you are unable to bear your measure of pain, unable to acknowledge life's insecurities and limitations, you see others as the cause. As Americans, we have a history of projecting our insecurity and fear onto a series of enemies du jour—the Communists, gays, blacks, Jews, Muslims, immigrants—and racism, intolerance, injustice, and war follow. Satirist P. J. O'Rourke writes, "One of the annoying things about believing in free will and individual responsibility is the difficulty of finding someone to blame your troubles on. When you do find somebody, it's remarkable how often his picture turns up on your driver's license."

Befriending the Trouble

The good news about these powerful inner forces is that you can use awareness to understand and tame them. When you mindfully recognize your fear, anger, desire, or loneliness, you come to know it, and then it begins to be workable. If you are lonely, for example, study it. The Sufi poet Hafiz warns, "Don't surrender your loneliness so quickly. Let it cut more deeply. Let it season you as few ingredients can." If you cannot bear your loneliness, your boredom, your anxiety, you will always run away. The moment you feel lonely or bored, you may open the fridge, or go online, or do anything to avoid being with yourself. But with loving awareness you can endure, honor, and value loneliness and aloneness. And they can be informative. They can teach you about yourself, your longings, what you have neglected for too long. They can help you find a deeper freedom.

Grief is the same. The Lakota Sioux value grief highly; they say it brings a person closer to the Great Spirit. When they want to send a message to the other side, they ask a member of a grieving family to deliver it. Whether you feel grief or anxiety, jealousy, addiction, or anger, your freedom grows by turning awareness toward it. Zen teacher Myogen Steve Stücky told his friends and students, when he was in great pain, dying of cancer, "I've found relief from suffering not by turning away but by turning toward what is most difficult."

In my own life, I've had to learn this with anger. My father was violent and abusive, a wife batterer who dominated all of our family with unpredictable outbursts of rage and paranoia. When he was most abusive, I would run away, and my mother hid bottles behind the curtains in every room so she could reach for one to defend herself against his blows.

I determined never to be like him. I became the family peacemaker, mediating arguments when I could. So, when I went to live as a young monk in a Thai forest monastery, I thought it would be easy and peaceful. I was unprepared for the intensity of my own restless mind, the uprising of grief, desire, and loneliness I felt. Most surprising was my anger. In not wanting to be like my violent father, I had suppressed all my anger—it had become dangerous even to feel. But in the awareness of meditation and solitude, all the things I was angry about came up. It was more than anger; it was fury. First at my father for being so hurtful to our family. Then, because it frightened me and I had denied it, I was angry at myself for all the times I had suppressed my anger.

Ajahn Chah told me to sit in the middle of it, to wrap myself in robes even on a hot day, and learn to tolerate it. Later my Reichian therapist had me breathe hard, make sounds, shout, grimace, rage, and flail, until I expressed fury's pain and wept. In these years of meditation and therapy I learned to work with the anger and discovered that it's an energy that can be known and tolerated, not feared. I had to acknowledge when it was present and realize that I *could* feel it fully without becoming vengeful or violent like my father.

I also realized that when understood, anger has value. It is a protest when we feel hurt or afraid or when our needs aren't met. At times, it even brings clarity. The ancient Greeks called anger a "noble" emotion, because it gives the strength to stand up for what you care most about. As I began to understand anger, I could see more clearly the frustration, hurt, and fear that were behind it. My sense of freedom grew as I became more intelligent about it, and slowly its energy was transformed into compassion for myself and others. Now I help others with their emotions as a part of my profession.

Resolving Conflicts

Arturo Bejar, a friend, served as one of the chief engineers at Facebook. His job included responding to problems and complaints by Facebook's members. He laughs when he points out that because Facebook is so huge, it doesn't take long for even 1 percent of users to register a million complaints. When they had engineering complaints, it was simple; Arturo sent them to Facebook's engineers to fix them. But many of the complaints were about interpersonal problems and about anger, resentment, blame, and hurt that had come up: "Someone posted a picture of me I don't like." "Someone posted a story about my kids, and they have no right to do so." "Someone wrote things about me that aren't quite right."

At first Facebook's response was to send out their legal policy, which explained that they would take down photos that were illegal, copyrighted, lewd, lascivious, et cetera. But Arturo saw that this policy left most people dissatisfied. He felt they needed to talk to each other. So, he began suggesting to users that, if they were unhappy with something another person did, they contact that person directly and try to sort it out. Then he realized they might need help with how to do this. "Tell them what you are concerned about." And then, to make the communication more complete, he also suggested, "Tell them how it made you feel."

Arturo then discovered that people often don't know how they feel, especially around difficulty. So, he suggested users learn to recognize their feelings. He even sent them emoticons to prompt their acknowledgment of feelings of hurt, confusion, worry, anger, sadness, fear, or not being appreciated. Finally, to further solve the conflict, Arturo suggested sending a simple inquiry, posing a question like "What made you post that?" or "What was your intention?"

The results were phenomenal. Eighty-five percent of the difficulties were resolved just by this process. Often the offender would respond, "I thought you looked good in this photo. Learning that it bothered you, of course I took it down." Or, "I'm sorry, I thought it would be fun to post about your kids." Arturo says,

"In this process, I get a chance to teach emotional intelligence and conflict resolution to 950 million people!"

Facing Demons

When you face the inner energies that most frighten, overwhelm, and bind you, it is important not to identify with them but to stay present with an observing mind that is not taking sides. Freedom dawns when you recognize the waves of emotions, see these energies for what they are, and you are not caught up in the dramatic stories your psyche has composed.

Wanting to be free from his own fear, the Buddha reflected in this way: "How would it be if, at the dark of the moon, I were to enter the most frightening places, near tombs and in the thick of the forest, that I might come to understand fear and terror. And being resolved to dispel the hold of fear, I did so, and remained facing that fear and terror until I was free of its hold upon me."

Tibetan master Milarepa is said to have put his head into the mouth of the worst demon that haunted him. A troubled young man I know named Marv told me that, after reading Milarepa, he decided to try the same approach. On a retreat, Marv said it was impossible for him to count how frequently the demons of anger, unworthiness, and self-destructive thoughts appeared to him. They had haunted him since his childhood. So, instead of rejecting them, he determined to stay in this deepest hell until he experienced and understood them fully. He surrendered to deliberately bring mindfulness and kindness to this suffering and fear, and meditated this way for some hours. Finally, at the very bottom of the well of pain, he saw a large ball that was emanating light. He entered it and immediately felt changed, released from his self-destructive fear for the first time in memory.

It happens this way. When we face our demons, whether boredom or shame, anger, judgment, or jealousy, they lose their power. We stop believing their story and start seeing them simply as human feelings. We stop wanting to get away or have something more, or feeling we did something wrong. Tori Murden, the first woman to row solo across the Atlantic, explains, "If you know what it means to be out in the middle of an ocean by yourself, in the dark, scared, then it gives you a feel for what every other human being is going through. I row an actual ocean. Other people have just as many obstacles to go through."

Believing that our worry and fear are real can drain us of vast amounts of energy. The poet Hafiz wrote, "Fear is the cheapest room in the house. I'd like to see you in better living conditions." If you pause for a moment, you'll see that fear is made of thoughts, and you can step aside and witness them as though they were anxious children. As you release fear, love and trust grow.

Dawn of Compassion

We all harbor troubling emotions. We all have shadows. Using awareness and compassion together can help us loosen their grip. Abiding in loving awareness, we become more spacious, and these unhealthy states begin to lose their power. As we learn to tolerate the feelings of pain, loss, and insecurity without expending all our energy to judge, retaliate, or push them away, a new feeling often arises. Freedom dawns as forgiveness and compassion enter your body and mind. Tibetan teacher Alan Wallace gives an example:

> *Imagine walking along a sidewalk with your arms full of groceries and someone roughly bumps into you so that you fall over and your groceries are strewn over the ground. As you rise up from the puddle of broken eggs and tomato juice, you are ready to shout out, "You idiot! What's wrong with you? Are you blind?" But just before you can catch your breath to speak, you see that the person who bumped into you actually is blind. He, too, is sprawled in the spilled groceries, and your anger vanishes in an instant, to be replaced by sympathetic concern: "Are you hurt? Can I help you up?" Our situation is like that. When we clearly realize that the source of disharmony and misery in the world is ignorance, we can open the door of wisdom and compassion.*

Sondra, a woman I worked with during a retreat, needed compassion to face her lifelong demon of binge eating. She described years of struggling with the compulsion, of wandering like a hungry ghost, full of self-hatred.

> *I believed that food had an unparalleled capacity to bring satisfaction and to free me from suffering. Time and again I have reached for the food, looking for it to do its magic, only to have it turn on me, fail*

*me, bring me untold physical and emotional suffering and shame. I
became hypercritical of myself and my situation, and then despaired.*

*Freedom has come as I have become more mindful of the intense
discomfort I was trying to escape from. I started to find that I could
recover more quickly and less painfully from bouts of compulsive
bingeing if I could stay even a little bit kind and present with my
pain. Instead of eating even more, just to try and avoid the effects
of having eaten too much and the remorse of having done it again,
I could actually watch myself start down that sad, old path. And as
the loving awareness grew, I realized, "Oh, I don't have to do this,"
and self-compassion could grow. I am deeply grateful for the compassion that has rescued me from the realm of the hungry ghosts.*

Sondra found that from kindness grew freedom. She realized she
was free to stop believing her destructive thoughts. And you are, too!

You do not have to identify with the unhealthy inner habits
that cause you pain. You are not your fear, your grasping, your
anger or confusion. With compassion and courage, difficult states
become empty phantoms, impostors, appearances that are not
real. In their stead, an inner world of well-being and balance
grows. Freedom is your true home.

PRACTICE

Compassion

To cultivate compassion, let yourself sit comfortably, in a centered and quiet way. Compassion practice combines phrases

of inner intention with visualization and the evocation of the feeling of compassion.

As you begin, breathe softly and feel your body, your heartbeat, the life within you. Feel how you treasure your own life, how you guard yourself in the face of dangers and sorrows. This is innate to all life. Now, bring to mind someone close to you whom you dearly love. Picture them and feel your natural caring for them. Notice how kindly you hold them. Then let yourself be aware of their struggles and fears, their troubles, their measure of sorrows, the suffering in their life, as in all human life. Feel how your heart naturally opens to wish them well, to extend comfort, to acknowledge their pain and meet it with compassion. This is the spontaneous response of the heart. As you picture them, inwardly recite these phrases:

May you be held in compassion.
May your pain and sorrow be eased.
May you be at peace.

Continue reciting these a number of times, all the while holding them in your heart. Let the feeling of compassion grow. Continue offering this caring intention for a time. You can modify these phrases in any way that makes them true to your heart's intention.

Then, after some minutes, imagine that this loved one is gazing back at you. Their eyes fill with the same spirit of compassion for your fears and troubles, your measure of sorrow and pain. They recite to you in return:

> *May you, too, be held in compassion.*
> *May your pain and sorrow be eased.*
> *May you be at peace.*

Take in their compassion and care. Now offer this same compassion to yourself. Hold your fears and troubles, suffering and pain in compassion. If you wish, put your hand on your heart. Recite the same phrases for a few minutes:

> *May I hold myself in compassion.*
> *May my pain and sorrow be eased.*
> *May I be at peace.*

Then, after a time, you can begin to extend compassion to others you know. Picture loved ones, one after another. Hold the image of each in your heart, be aware of their difficulties, and wish them well with the same phrases.

Next you can open your compassion further, a step at a time, to the suffering of your friends, to your neighbors, to your community. You can gradually extend your compassion to all who suffer, to difficult people, to your enemies, and finally to the brotherhood and sisterhood of all beings. Sense your tenderhearted connection with all life and its creatures.

Work with compassion practice intuitively. At times, it may

feel difficult, you might be afraid of being overwhelmed by the pain. Remember, you are not trying to "fix" the pain of the world, only to meet it with a compassionate heart. Relax and be gentle. Breathe. Let your breath and heart rest naturally, as a center of great compassion in the midst of the world.

PRACTICE
Practice with Troubled Emotions

To practice with troubled emotions, sit quietly and choose a circumstance where you feel stuck. Notice the difficult emotions that are present, often making your problems worse. Observe kindly whatever troubled emotions are present. Breathe and let the emotions be. Fear and frustration, anxiety and worry, anger and rage, loneliness and sorrow may be there . . . are all natural to human life. Turn toward them. Feel how they manifest in your body, your heart, and your mind. With loving awareness, simply acknowledge, "Fear feels like this," "Frustration feels like this," "Pain feels like this." Already by naming them you become the mindful witnessing, the loving awareness.

After a minute or two, focus on one of these difficult emotions. Acknowledge whatever it is: "Anger feels like this." "____ feels like this." Notice where it is centered in your body. Now invite the emotion or feeling to become stronger, to expand and increase. Feel yourself making space for it to grow as big as it wants. Let it open and fill your whole body. Then sense or feel or imagine it expanding further, to fill the room, the space around you, the whole sky. Let the emotion or feeling grow vast. Take your time. As the feeling expands, notice what happens to it. At first it may intensify and grow stronger. Then, as it expands even further, it often becomes softer, and the energy of this emotion opens to other experiences. Sometimes it begins to feel less personal. It becomes simply an energy of anger, of fear, of loneliness moving through you. Sometimes as it softens, another strong feeling arises, anger makes way for sadness or hurt, loneliness gives birth to worry or to tenderness. The energy becomes more universal and can even open to its opposite. You may also notice that as you allow these energies to open, you become less reactive. Their energy is freed to move. Now you can be present and gracious but not so easily caught or swept away.

Of course, some feelings return many times, reappearing like waves. Let them come and go. Do not be discouraged. They are the energy of life, come to teach you. They arise from how much you have been hurt or afraid, are vulnerable, and how much you care, and they can lead you to a more universal, deep tender concern and compassion. Trust this process. It is healing and liberating to the heart.

Part Three

Realizing Freedom

*You are not yet free. You have merely
achieved the freedom to be free.*

—NELSON MANDELA

Chapter 8

Elegance of Imperfection

It was the touch of the imperfect upon the would-be
perfect that gave the sweetness, because it was that
which gave the humanity.

—THOMAS HARDY, *TESS OF THE D'URBERVILLES*

We have so many ideas about how we should be and how the world should be, yet none of these is the way things are. Human life is a tainted glory—messy, paradoxical, filled with contradictions. The cloak of the world is woven with magnificence *and* limitation, triumph and disappointment, loss and eternal re-creation. To seek some ideal of perfection puts us in conflict with the world.

Invitation to Care

David Roche, a teacher and humorist who founded the Church of 80% Sincerity, says 80% is good enough: 80% wise, 80% compassionate, 80% celibate. David was born with a huge tumor on the bottom left side of his face; surgeons tried to remove it when he was very young and, in the process, removed his lower lip, and gave him such extensive radiation that the lower part of his face stopped growing, and he was covered with plum-colored burns.

Now he lectures at middle schools about imperfection. When he walks in and takes the stage, he is aware that many of the kids can't bear to look at him. Self-conscious teens obsess and fear that their own bodies are flawed. David puts it, "Here I am, your worst nightmare." He asks them to imagine going to a party with this face, or what it's like getting in an elevator where parents say to their kids, "Shush, don't say anything." Sometimes he jokes that he is tempted to respond, "It all happened because I touched my wee-wee."

David is funny and truthful, poignant and fearless about his disabilities, and so wise that little by little his stories and his heart win over the students. Sometimes his lovely wife, Marlena, is with him. At the end of most of his talks, he asks the audience to look at him again and see if he looks any different. He does, they say. Now they can see him, his humanity, his heart. He shows them what it means to love your glorious, imperfect self.

Tyranny of Perfection

For Emily, who had a history of depression and anxiety, finding the freedom of imperfection required befriending shame and confusion, which she saw as a figure named Mara. In stories of the

Buddha in India, Mara is the embodiment of greed, hate, and ignorance who fought with the Buddha on the night of his awakening and for years after. Each time Mara attacked him, the Buddha remained unmoved and simply said, "I see you, Mara," and Mara would throw up his hands at being recognized and skulk away. In some later accounts, the Buddha even invited his old friend Mara over for tea.

Mara appeared to Emily in the form of shame and confusion. Whenever money was tight, work difficult, whenever she gained a couple of pounds or her ex-boyfriend called, Mara would attack her. It was a familiar pattern. From childhood, Emily held a sense that something was wrong with her. "I'm not charming, good-looking, smart, creative, or fast enough." Her list went on and on.

Gradually, through her practice of mindfulness and loving awareness, Emily gained a more spacious perspective and was able to see Mara clearly. To do this, she first learned to feel her ever-changing breath and witness her body's aches and pains with equanimity and kindness. Then she learned to sit with and be curious about the different states, the guises of Mara that visited her mind and heart. She learned to name them as the Buddha had: "Oh, Mara of despair, Mara of shame, is that you again? I see you." Then she learned to compassionately decline their grasp. "Even if you want to have tea, I can't let you stay too long because I have another engagement."

We long for perfection. The perfect partner, house, job, boss, and spiritual teacher. And when we find them, we want them to stay that way forever, never to lose the glow, never to grow old, never to have the roof sag, the paint peeling. We're also taught to seek perfection in ourselves. Novelist Florida Scott-Maxwell writes, "No matter how old a mother is, she looks at her middle-age children for signs of improvement." You are told that if you do enough therapy, work out at the gym, eat an especially healthy diet, watch documentaries on TV, manage your cholesterol, and meditate enough, you will become more perfect.

Forget the tyranny of perfection. The point is not to perfect yourself. It is to perfect your love. Let your imperfections be an invitation to care. Remember that imperfections are deliberately woven into Navajo rugs and treasured in the best Japanese pottery. They are part of the art. What a relief to honor your life as it is, in all its beauty and imperfection.

Wild, Uncharted, Imperfect Glory

We imagine that if we become really spiritual, we will never be afraid or angry, or even grieve or fret. We want to live in the world yet be untouched by challenges, projecting a wise and loving Buddha-like veneer, living with perfect peace.

We glorify leaders, artists, and spiritual teachers. Yet they all have aspects that don't fit our idealization. Like everyone else, great spiritual teachers experience conflict and trouble with those around them. Buddha did. So did Jesus, the Dalai Lama, and Mother Teresa. They also get migraines, backaches, diabetes, heart conditions, depression. Beloved masters like Suzuki Roshi, the 16th Karmapa, and Ramana Maharshi all died of cancer. The awakened heart is not found through some ideal of perfection, but by bringing love to it all: praise and blame, gain and loss, joy and sorrow.

There is a difference between an archetype or ideal and our humanity. Gandhi and Martin Luther King Jr., Krishnamurti and Chögyam Trungpa had shadows. Lamas and mamas, bishops and rabbis, all wrestle with their own imperfections. Even someone as wonderful as the Dalai Lama says, "Sometimes I get angry, but then I realize, what's the use, and let it go."

Some years ago, I studied in a group with the oldest and most senior Rinzai Zen master in the West, Joshu Sasaki Roshi. We sat for seemingly endless, sometimes painful hours in long rows, Zen-style, not moving, meditating on koans, the apparently impossible-to-answer questions he gave each of us. I was already a well-known meditation teacher at the time, and in my first retreat with him, he gave me what I thought was a difficult koan.

Each of us students went in separately to see him four times a day. After a ceremonial bow and a recitation of our koan, we were to demonstrate our answer. I tried one answer after another, and after each response, Roshi would look at me and say, "No," or "Good idea but not Zen," or "Not quite," and ring the bell for me to leave. After I spent days and nights trying harder and harder (a mistake), the master's amusement graduated to ridicule. "Too much ego" or "Two percent," he would say, and then ask, "You a teacher?" and "No good." I gave every kind of answer I could think of and became more and more frustrated.

One evening after many such encounters, I became fed up,

angry at him, myself, the whole process. As I kept reciting my koan, I just let myself be angry. By the time the gong sounded to get in line to see the master, I was furious and I thought, He's a Zen Master. Let's see what he does with a really angry student. So, I went in, bowed, and he asked me to recite my koan. I shouted "Fuck you, Roshi!" smashed out the candle on his table with my palm, picked up his bell, rang it myself, and stormed out. As I turned the door handle, I heard him ring the bell again and say calmly and in a bemused tone, "No. Not the answer."

After that, I gave up trying to do it right, and of course, as in all Zen stories, my mind softened, the koan became more natural, and the answer just appeared. By the end of the retreat, as much as I was pleased by learning to work with koans, I was even more moved by how the process also included my frustration, doubt, humiliation, and confusion, as well as a full-blown tantrum. The answer was not apart from this messy process, but opening in the midst of it all. Honoring every messy part of life and still sitting is Zen.

If you want to explore imperfection and love, take off your clothes and look in a full-length mirror. Notice the mysterious gift of having a human body and a human life. And notice all the ideas of how it should be. Can you see and love your body, and your human life, clearly as it is? With all its unique, messy, wild, uncharted, imperfect glory?

Eyes of Love

One woman I knew who had taken up Zen had an obvious and visible problem in her practice: she was born with the lower half of an arm missing and could not create the mudra, one palm on the other resting on her lap, which Zen posture requires. Perhaps because it was awkward and embarrassing to mention it (what if this were me?), none of the young meditation hall instructors talked to her about it. Still, she practiced sincerely and became more silent and open to her life. Partway through one Zen retreat, she was in her room looking in the mirror and realized, with compassion and chagrin, "I've never really looked at my arm!" She was twenty-six years old and had never looked at herself without judgment, dismay, or even revulsion. Like David Roche, the cancer survivor whose face was disfigured by radiation treatments, she had visible damage to her body, but the real damage was to her spirit, which she had not seen. Only by embracing our imperfection can we become free. Then our vision becomes *pure perception,* seeing with the eyes of love.

In 1971, Ram Dass, who became the author of the bestselling *Be Here Now,* was encouraged by his guru Neem Karoli Baba to return to the United States from India to teach. His guru's message was one of love: "Love people and feed them." Ram Dass was hesitant; he protested to Neem Karoli Baba that he felt too impure and spiritually imperfect to teach. His guru got up from his wooden seat, took several minutes to circle Ram Dass slowly and carefully, peering at him from all sides, then sat back down. Looking Ram Dass deeply in the eyes, he said simply, "I see no imperfections." Ram Dass returned to America, bringing the teaching of pure love to millions.

You are perfectly yourself. The gifts you seek of love and compassion are not in faraway India. They are always here waiting for you. I see the fruit of loving awareness and self-compassion become visible at the end of retreats. On the first days, the meditators' busy minds begin to settle. Gradually their minds quiet, their bodies open, their eyes soften. They become less hurried, more present to themselves and the world. People sometimes joke about the *vipassana face-lift,* because meditators leave retreats looking younger and more alive. Whenever you see with the eyes of love, everything changes.

What You Have Left

Still, it's hard not to look at your life and compare it to the ideals on magazine covers of celebrities, supermodels, and Olympic athletes. You can easily feel less than they are. As a worried middle school student, a harried manager, or a struggling parent, you can wonder whether you measure up—are you good enough? This ideal is an imaginary fiction. In fact, at home, celebrities don't look like they do on magazine covers, and they struggle with life—with their aging bodies, their families, managing their money. Just like all humans, they face praise and blame, joy and sorrow, gain and loss. To have compassion for your human vulnerability is a blessed, tender practice. Poet Alison Luterman calls her life a "wonderful failure."

When astronauts return to earth they are so grateful just to breathe the fresh air, to walk on the ground, to celebrate being home. This earth, this history, this body are yours. Feel the joy and sorrow that make up your incarnation. Yes, you want to protect yourself, but remember, your sorrow will teach you compassion. Your vulnerability will bring tenderness, and the renewal of each day will bring you joy. Appreciation of your wonderful, messy failures of life will bring you peace.

Get comfortable in your own skin. Practice compassion for yourself. Care for the garden you have been given, accept it, tend it with love. Zen Master Suzuki Roshi summed it up, "You are perfect just the way you are. And there is still room for improvement." Love yourself. This is the essence. Then take your very human imperfections and make beauty anyway.

Itzhak Perlman, one of the world's greatest violinists, demonstrates this. Perlman was stricken with polio as a child; he has braces on both his legs and walks with two crutches. He crosses the stage slowly, yet majestically, until he reaches his chair. Then he sits down lowers his crutches to the floor, undoes the clasps on his legs, bends down and picks up the violin, puts it under his chin, nods to the conductor, and proceeds to play.

But one time at a concert at Avery Fisher Hall at Lincoln Center in New York City, something went wrong. In the middle of the concert, one of the strings on his violin broke. You could hear it snap—it went off like a gunshot. There was no mistaking what that sound meant: he would not be able to play the piece as it was written on his violin. People who were there wondered whether he'd have to put on the braces and go backstage—to find another violin or another string. But he didn't. Instead, he waited a moment, closed his eyes, and then signaled the conductor to begin again. The orchestra began, and Perlman played on only three strings, modulating the piece in his head and adapting it to use the remaining strings with passion, steadiness, and remarkable purity.

When he finished, an awed silence filled the room. Then people stood and applause rose from every corner of the auditorium, bravos and cheering. Perlman smiled, wiped the sweat from his brow, raised his bow to quiet the audience, and then he said—not boastfully, but in a quiet, pensive, reverent tone—"You know, sometimes it is your task in life to find out how much music you can still make with what you have left."

Mastery

When we encounter the best of humanity—the best violinist, the best accordion player, the best rodeo rider, the best astrophysicist, the best rose gardener—it is inspiring. The best artists and performers have probably practiced many more than the ten thousand hours Malcolm Gladwell says are required for mastery. When you hear a musical genius such as Yo-Yo Ma or Stevie Wonder or watch an Olympic gymnast such as Simone Biles, you see what is close to human perfection. Their best is a combination of their prodigious gifts and profound dedication. And while they may be the best at their special art, in other areas they are undoubtedly undeveloped. Even a brilliant actor such as

Sir Laurence Olivier found himself grappling with lifelong, overwhelming stage fright.

It is natural to admire and celebrate excellence and the dedication that goes with it. Choosing to give yourself fully to an art, a work, a creation, a discipline is part of your human freedom, joyful and admirable. Dedication and commitment help you give your best, hone your skills, commit to your art, your work, your love. But they and their results are different from perfection. Artists, parents, athletes, chefs may celebrate their best performances, their best meals with satisfaction. But if they are obsessed with holding on to perfection, they will suffer—and lose their edge. Dedication and giving totally are what bring joy. Otherwise as actor Dustin Hoffman says, "Every good review is simply a stay of execution."

The classic examples of this kind of suffering are the overly ambitious parents at Little League and soccer matches. Wanting to make their children into future stars and craving the reflected glory, the parents rant and push. Their obsession robs the game of the spirit of play and enjoyment that make it, and life, worth playing.

Dedication and commitment are beautiful qualities that are best tempered by love and wisdom. You can set your goals, direct your energy, work with vigor, and try for the best, but the results are always uncertain. The most magnificent performances are ephemeral, the best of art is a beautiful statement, and then life moves on. Freedom requires dedication and commitment, but not clinging to the result.

It's Already Broken

Everything in this world is subject to change and renewal. We are a flow of yin and yang, of sense experiences and dreams, an ever-changing river of feelings and thoughts. Consistency is the realm of the press release; inconsistency is the stuff of life. Relax. Hold the paradox of change and eternity with grace rather than judgment or fear. Then you will see that in this imperfect world, there is another kind of joy. We have the ability to be perfectly ourselves. We have the laughter of the wise, the freedom to choose our spirit no matter the circumstances. We have the freedom to love anyway. To love amid the glorious, terrifying, and unshakable beauty of it all. We have the wisdom and courage to care sweetly in this fleeting, evanescent play of days.

Ajahn Chah held up his favorite Chinese teacup and said, "To me, this cup is already broken. Because I know this, I can drink from it and appreciate it fully. And when it falls off the table, I understand. It's the way things are."

Reality demands flexibility. You can backtrack, repeat, change your mind, learn a new way, bend, sway, lose it and find it, try another gate, turn around, follow another path, do everything in moderation, including moderation. You can learn to be present with curiosity and discover what happens next.

Discover the ease of making mistakes, trusting, failing, letting yourself be carried by something larger than yourself. When Rossini was composing his great chorus in G minor, he accidentally dipped his pen in a medicine bottle instead of the inkpot. "It made a blot, and when I dried it with sand [blotting paper had not yet been invented], it took the form of a natural, which instantly gave me the idea of the effect which the change from G Minor to G Major would make, and to this blot all the beautiful effect of the chorus is due."

With the freedom of imperfection comes forgiveness and compassion for yourself and others. A young army officer who had a hot temper and a history of anger and stress-related problems was ordered by his colonel to attend an eight-week mindfulness training to reduce his level of stress. One day, after attending classes for several weeks, he stopped for groceries on his way home. He was in a hurry and a bit irritated, as he often was. When he took his cart to check out, there were long lines. He noticed the woman in front of him had only one item but wasn't in the express line. She was carrying a baby, and as she got to the cashier, they stopped to talk. He became irritated. She was in the wrong line, talking, and holding everyone up. How selfish, he thought. Then she passed the baby to the cashier and the cashier spent a moment cooing over the child. He could feel his anger rising. But because he'd been practicing mindfulness, he started to become aware of the heat and tightness in his body, and he could feel the pain. He breathed and relaxed. When he looked up again he saw the little boy smiling. As he reached the cashier, he said, "That was a cute little boy." She responded, "Oh, did you like him? That's my baby. His father was in the Air Force, but he was killed last winter. Now I have to work full-time. My mom tries to bring my boy in once or twice a day so I can see him."

We are so quick to judge. But it needn't be this way. Look anew at the world around you. With mindfulness, you can see with the eyes of care and wonder. The philosopher Nietzsche describes how, beyond our ideas and ideals, our hearts can open. "Out of the abyss of great suspicion, one returns newborn having shed one's skin, more ticklish and sarcastic, with a more delicious taste for joy, with a more tender tongue for all good things, with gayer senses, with a second dangerous innocence in joy, more childlike and yet a hundred times subtler than one has ever seen before." This is an invitation to freedom.

PRACTICE
I See You, Mara

Mara, the mythological embodiment of greed, hatred, and ignorance, has a way of regularly visiting all humans. A master of many guises, Mara knows just how to hook you. Mara can appear as fear or self-doubt, or transform into addictive temptation or righteous aggression. You have your personalized Mara who visits. Like the Top 10 tunes on the radio, Mara will have some favorite forms. First, you must learn to recognize them as aspects of Mara. They might be shame or confusion, irritation or anxiety, anger or self-hate. They often have an idealistic underpinning, telling you how you should be better, smarter, thinner, wiser. Or they tell you how other people should be.

You can give Mara's most frequent forms a funny name or a number. Maybe the top visitors will be shame or self-criticism, worry or anger. "Oh, Mara number two, I see you." "Oh, Anxious Mara, I see you." Use humor and spacious, loving awareness. "Even if you want to visit, I can't let you stay too long; I have another engagement." Even as Mara presses his views, stay steady and kind. You can treat Mara with compassion, but you don't have to binge with him. He is an old friend, and all he needs to hear is, "I see you, Mara." Your true identity is loving awareness, and whenever you acknowledge, "I see you, Mara," Mara loses his power, and you step into freedom.

PRACTICE

Practicing Imperfection

What if you could love yourself fully, including your imperfections? What if you could love others in the same way?

You might fear that by loving your anger or laziness, your addictions or your anxiety, you would never change for the better. That you would become more angry and lazier or more addicted and self-centered.

But if you experiment, you will see that what happens is often the opposite. As you love and accept yourself in a bigger, wiser love, your fear and aggression, your neediness and inertia lose their hold. Your love knows intuitively what is in your best interest, a love warmed by the sacredness of the heart's affections.

Try it. Sit quietly and invite a sense of presence and loving awareness just where you are. After a time, let yourself reflect: become aware of what you consider your imperfections and flaws.

First, reflect on how you see your body. What are its flaws and imperfections?

Second, reflect in the same way on your personality and character. What are its main imperfections and flaws?

Then reflect on your mind states and the imperfections you find there. Include the imperfections in your relationships with others.

Imagine you were to love yourself just as you are—with all these human flaws. Every human has imperfections; this is part of human incarnation. Your task is to see them clearly and love anyway.

Now become the loving awareness that can witness and hold your life with its successes and imperfections in a sea of love. Who you are is not the flaws and trauma and fears. These are outer human struggles appearing in pure consciousness. You are timeless awareness, born with original beauty, the child of the spirit having a complicated human incarnation, like the other seven billion of us.

With this deep acceptance and loving awareness, step out of the judge's court. Invite yourself to become quiet, at ease with your whole self, kind and thoughtful. With this accepting presence, you will see yourself make better choices—not out of shame or self-hate, but because your loving heart teaches you how to care. The loving heart transforms the whole human dance.

After you practice embracing your imperfections in this way, you can choose other people with imperfections to include in this practice. Start with easy ones first, then some harder ones.

See and accept all their imperfections with a profound loving awareness. Take your time. Notice how this acceptance changes your conflicts and feelings for the better. Other people are learners, just as you are. And when you envision loving them with all their flaws, notice how your loving gaze and care might inspire the best in them. As Nelson Mandela says, "It never hurts to see the good in someone. They often act the better because of it."

Chapter 9

The Gift of an Open Mind

Now there's a man with an open mind—you
can feel the breeze from here.

—GROUCHO MARX

J ust as your lungs expand and contract, so does your mind. The mind investigates the world by organizing an ever-changing river of sense data into perceptions, establishing a sense of self and other, time and perspective, meaning, values, and ideas. We rely on these perceptions and past experiences to order our world. When the mind is open, we see clearly, discover, enjoy, and respond to life. When we have a closed mind, the world becomes small, frightening, and rigid. Keep in mind that whatever perspective you hold, it is just that—one view among many, seen from a limited angle.

Zen and the Art of Openness

At a retreat on the Big Sur Coast, I invited several visiting masters and lamas. Kobun Chino Roshi, a Zen Master, taught about being open to many possibilities, then he offered to demonstrate the famous art of Zen Archery. On the appointed afternoon, he set up his target at the west end of an elegant lawn, which dropped off into the Pacific Ocean. The retreatants and teachers gathered, and the Roshi made a beautiful shrine on a nearby rock, where he offered prayers. Then slowly and with exquisite care, like a ballet, he bowed and changed into an outer white silk robe. He raised and unsheathed his bow from its leather case and carefully strung it. Then he uncased the arrows, sat meditating with them in his lap, then spun them and looked down the length from feathers to tip, finally selecting one. He stood and mindfully paced fifty feet from the target. There he rested—alert, silent, present.

The spectators were hushed. After what seemed like a long time, he raised his bow and then notched the arrow. He turned toward the target, stood, very slowly drew the arrow fully back, aimed, and after a long time deliberately raised the bow higher and let the arrow fly. And it flew—over the target, over the cliff, into the ocean. Success. He smiled broadly. Then he took another fifteen minutes in elegant fashion to gracefully unstring the bow, pack the arrows, bow to the altar, and change into his black robe. At the end, he laughed and bowed to us all.

When Evan's cousin got engaged to an Egyptian Muslim woman he'd met in college, Evan decided to visit them. Evan and the couple met in a café and, when Evan saw his cousin's fiancée in a headscarf, prejudices flooded his mind. He'd never actually known a Muslim, so when she turned out to be funny, warm, open-minded, and intelligent, he was shocked. He felt foolish about stereotyping and writing off one-fifth of humanity.

A similar change of mind happened to Sandra, a high school teacher, when she was transferred to an urban school filled with tattooed gang kids. Their baggy pants and tough talk, the posturing and attitude, the violence she'd read about and seen on TV scared her. Until then, she'd always crossed the street to avoid people like them. But after six months of teaching these young men and women, her perception changed. She learned about the lives and struggles of Pedro, Vinh, and Malcolm; they became real people to her. Now she would cross the street toward them just to say hello. And they would say, "Yo, Sandra, what's up?" They had become her guys.

Prejudice and Perspective

Nobel Prize–winning researchers David Hubel and Torsten Wiesel demonstrated how powerful perceptual conditioning can be in a study in which newborn kittens were divided into three groups, each placed in a different environment during the critical few days when they were opening their eyes and sight was developing. The first group was placed in a white box painted with horizontal black stripes, the second in a white box with vertical black stripes, and the third in a pure white box. The imprinting of those first days stayed with the kittens for life. Those raised in a world with only horizontal stripes could not properly see anything vertical. They routinely ran into chair and table legs, which they literally could not perceive. The kittens raised in a vertical world could not see horizontal lines. The kittens raised in an all-white world were even more disoriented and had difficulty moving around any object correctly.

Depending on your perspective, you can see a cow as a milk producer, as meat, as leather, as a mother, an ungulate, a farm animal, a Hindu holy being, or a living mystery. If you see a cow only as meat or as an investment, a great deal is lost from your perception. The same is true with people, with cultures, in every circumstance of life. You can see, caught by your desires and opinions, or you can look with new eyes and experience the freedom that is patiently waiting for you. What a joy to meet the world with an open mind. It's a two-way gift—a gift of freedom to you and a blessing to others.

Yet there is also pain in seeing clearly. We have ignored some areas of life in order to avoid being in conflict or feeling overwhelmed. Turning away can hide loss, injustice, addiction, superficiality, intolerance. To see clearly takes courage. When Ram Dass taught a class on compassion and service in Oakland, California, he asked the students to pay attention to their responses to the suffering around them. One woman reported that she had given money to a neighborhood homeless man every time she passed him for months, but she never looked too closely. Now she realized why: "If I ever really look in his eyes, I'm afraid the next thing I know he will be sleeping on my living room couch."

You don't have to bring the homeless and all the world's suffering into your home, but you do have to learn to see them clearly and hold them in your heart. Over time this woman became an ally to her neighbor, this homeless man, and her care and charity changed both of their lives. You have to be tender with the wounds and traumas of the world, and of your own life. Opening your heart slowly, gently, carefully, you can listen to the way things really are with interest and care, and see in a way that is curious, fresh, and kind.

An open mind allows the vibrancy of living in the moment. In theater, no matter how brilliant an actor is, he will always be upstaged when a child or a dog comes onstage. We love seeing what is surprising and unscripted. Spontaneity, creativity, aliveness are hallmarks of a free, open mind. Kobun Chino's teacher Suzuki Roshi famously said, "In the beginner's mind, there are many possibilities; in the expert's, there are few."

When you are open-minded in the present, notice how your direct experience is invariably different from your idea about it. A person is always more interesting, multidimensional, and unexpected than your preconceptions. Your memory of a cousin or perspective about a leader often melts away when you meet them in person. What would happen if you held your perspectives more lightly?

You may choose to look at the world as a conservative, a liberal, or a libertarian, as a scientist or a fundamentalist; you may see it as a fearful place or a celebration of creativity. Remember respect. Each of these perspectives has value, and yet each is only a partial truth. When you are rigid in your beliefs, you will suffer.

As the Buddha noted, "Those who cling to their views go about the world annoying people." Open-mindedness is the antidote.

Breaking Barriers

After the first group of Westerners at Ajahn Chah's monastery arrived, and then many more appeared, some local villagers suggested they create a nearby forest monastery where teachings could be offered in English. Quite successful, the strict and yet loving teaching at this new temple inspired the ordination of Western monks and nuns from many backgrounds. One American nun, sincere and charismatic, became well regarded, a favorite in the local villages as her command of Thai and Lao grew. But then, after five years, she abruptly left without explanation.

Saddened by her departure, they were surprised when she returned a year later, an evangelical Christian. Now a laywoman, she stayed at the monastery and spent her days exhorting the residents and nearby villagers to turn to Christ. After a time, this became unsettling and distressing to many of them. Wanting to make a strong response to her unsuitable activity, they decided to consult with Ajahn Chah. A group of monks and village laypeople walked the ten miles through the forest to the main monastery. Seated with the master, they described the situation and how upsetting it was to them to hear her preaching the Gospel in their Buddhist temple. The situation was not news to Ajahn Chah—others had told him about her proselytizing. "How can we let her do this?" they asked. Can we make her be silent or force her to leave? The group wanted to send her packing.

Ajahn Chah listened to every word of their distress. Then he smiled broadly. "Well," he said, "maybe she's right."

Almost everyone laughed. They understood how tightly they were holding their Buddhist views and the suffering that flowed from that attachment. He sent them back, some smiling, some sighing. After she was no longer meeting resistance, the ex-nun stayed a short while longer and then left.

Talitha's mother was a strong southern conservative and her father a Republican businessman. When Talitha became involved in a yoga and meditation community, her parents were worried, even though yoga was also offered at their country club. When she came home to visit, they got into arguments about immigration, abortion, religion—all the hot-button issues. It made every visit unpleasant and blocked the family's love from expressing itself.

Then Talitha fell in love with Jeff, a strong, thoughtful man in Washington who treated her wonderfully and was also a real conservative. In lengthy conversations, they tried to convince each other of their own perspectives, and because they were open-hearted and in love, they really listened to each other. As a result, the next time Talitha returned home for a family visit, she was more open-minded. Talitha's parents didn't change their views, but somehow the conversation softened on both sides—from adversarial to one of shared concern. And with this, the gate of love reopened and Talitha felt she could be in an honest conversation and not just the repetitive conflicts of the past.

When you see how you cling to views, you break the spell of misperception and regain connection.

Of course, it's natural to have views. The question is: Do they close your mind and your heart? You may have views about bankers, atheists, boomers, evangelicals, feminists, or lawyers. You may have views of other people's politics, religion, way of life, or way of dressing. You think you know who they are. Freedom requires you to ask yourself, "Why am I holding this fixed view? What else about them is also true?"

Look at the next person who comes through the door with fresh, innocent eyes. Who are they really? What are their dreams? What is the depth of their heart? What is ahead for them? What is their gift? These kinds of questions can change the way you think about others and, since most of your preconceptions are really projections, how you think about yourself.

Are You Sure?

I love the startling moments when I realize that I've been seeing things all wrong. I have spent many months in Bali, home to thousands of beautiful Hindu temples and a rich tradition of sacred dance and collective daily ritual. On a recent trip, I was visiting a renowned painter's village in the late afternoon, and I walked down a tree-lined path to one of the biggest temples on the village outskirts. Behind a four-foot-high carved stone wall, I could see fifty figures dressed in white, heads bobbing up and down, in what I thought must be a big temple ceremony. I walked closer, wanting to see this beautiful ritual. It was only when I got close and could hear the music and peer over the wall that I realized the ancient sacred ceremony I expected was in fact an aerobics class.

"We see the world not as it is," says the Talmud, "but as we are." When Samuel Burke, who was blind from the age of ten months, got his sight back at age fifty, he was astonished by the appearance of a crescent moon and asked what it was. He had always imagined that the quarter moon would look like a quarter piece of cake. Like Samuel, we all have erroneous ideas. Sometimes we cling to them deliberately. "Don't introduce me to him," said the renowned essayist Charles Lamb about a man he disliked. "I want to go on hating him, and I can't hate a man I know."

When your mind is closed, you lose a true connection to others and fall into defensiveness, rigidity, fear, and conflict. In the worst case, you fool yourself and live a lie. Michael Ventura explains:

> *The people you have to lie to, own you. The things you have to lie about, own you. When your children see that you are owned, then they are not your children anymore, they are the children of what owns you. If money owns you, they are the children of money. If your need for pretense and illusion owns you, they are the children of pretense and illusion. If your fear of loneliness owns you, they are the children of loneliness. If your fear of the truth owns you, they are the children of the fear of truth.*

Actually See Her

When I've sat at the bedsides of folks at the end of life, sometimes I hear regrets: for the ways they failed to live their dreams, failed to speak their truth, or failed to love well in spite of it all. I am struck by the honesty and tenderness of this time, the willingness to undertake what the twelve-step work calls "a fearless moral inventory" of our life.

But you do not have to wait until the end of life to see clearly. Even today you can look clearly with courage, unafraid to see your own faults and to make changes and amends. You can look anew.

An Indonesian man, falsely imprisoned, implored his wife to smuggle in a hacksaw or some tool to escape. But she was forbidden to see him and allowed to send only a prayer rug. For weeks, he was despondent. Why didn't she send him something of use? Then one day, staring at the rug, he noticed that his wife had woven into the rug a diagram of how to escape.

Closed-mindedness is a prison. The love and freedom you seek are your birthright. Open your eyes and discover they are here, waiting for you to step out of your fixed views and notice.

At a Berkeley conference on mindfulness and the law, I heard these instructions from a judge to a jury:

I want you to listen to what will be presented in this courtroom with total attention. You may find it helpful to sit in a posture that embodies dignity and presence, and to stay in touch with the feeling of your breath moving in and out of your body as you listen to the evidence. Be aware of the tendency for your mind to jump to conclusions before all the evidence has been presented and final arguments made. As best you can, continually try to suspend judgment and simply witness with your full being everything that is being presented in the courtroom moment by moment by moment. If you find your mind wandering a lot, you can always bring it back to your breathing and to what you are hearing, over and over again if necessary. When the presentation of evidence is complete, then it will be your turn to deliberate together as a jury and come to a decision. But not before.

When you meet someone, actually *see* them—as they are today. When you talk with someone who has a different perspective, listen openly and you'll connect in surprising ways.

Encounter every new moment with wonder and gratitude, and you'll experience that it's never too late to open your mind and your heart. As Bob Dylan sings, "He who's not being born is busy dying." Live fully and freely.

The Healing Power of Words

Words have enormous power. They start journeys, marriages, movies, lawsuits, and wars. And they end them. We talk to infants in the womb, and the river of words continues even after a person's last breath. Like waves of water, words can injure and separate or connect and heal.

A renowned healer was once called in to say special prayers for a sick child whose medicine was slow to work. After offering the prayers, the healer pronounced, "Now she will be well." A skeptical bystander scoffed that simply saying prayers was nonsense and did nothing. The master healer turned toward the skeptic and said, "You are dressed like an ignorant peasant, and your words are spoken like a real fool." The bystander immediately became upset and was about to respond in anger when the healer said, "Just a moment now. If a few words can so quickly turn you red and angry, why shouldn't other words have the power to heal?"

While I was working in support of peacemakers in Palestine and Israel, one of the programs I visited brought together teenagers from both sides. After three summers of shared camps, projects, arguments, dances, and dialogues, the teens invited their parents to meet. It was a tense time politically, but permits were arranged for the Palestinian parents to join the other families in Israel. I stood in a circle at the camp with one of the groups of teens. They had become close friends and held hands. Their parents stood in a circle behind them, gazing at the connection the teens had created. Then one of the Palestinian mothers spoke softly: "For twenty years, the only Israelis I've seen have been soldiers. I forgot they had mothers, too."

When you approach others with expectations, demands, and stereotypes, you don't connect. At best, you get a superficial exchange, and often you get defensiveness or even conflict. Happiness grows from an open mind.

With openness, you can approach conversations, family, friends and enemies, creativity, and conflict with a willingness to listen and learn rather than just defend yourself. An open mind brings empathetic listening that can foster understanding no matter how great the differences. This doesn't mean you will agree with others or neglect your own boundaries. It is simple. Open-minded speech is both true and useful, caring and attuned. It means entering into conversation interested, wanting to comprehend the other's circumstance and perspective. This openness has an enormous impact, whether in relationships, community building, or politics.

Heartfelt Communication

A group of British antinuclear activists had been demonstrating, some quite angrily for months, against the deployment of more missiles. The leaders of the group felt they were protecting millions of people and other forms of life from grave potential disaster. Finally, after long negotiations, the leaders of the group were invited to meet with the senior NATO general under whose command the nuclear missiles were being kept. The night before their meeting, the woman who led their delegation realized that if they began by confronting the general for this destructive and homicidal policy, the meeting would escalate, polarize their positions, and lead nowhere. She had a revelation: the general must feel that he, too, was protecting millions of people. The next morning, when they opened the meeting, she began, "It must be difficult to feel responsible to protect so many millions of lives." "It is," he replied. And this was the start of a very productive dialogue in which the general himself shared thoughts on how to reduce the number of missiles.

Heartfelt and free communication begins with loving attention to yourself and the other. Articulated in the brilliant work of Marshall Rosenberg called Nonviolent Communication, it fosters sensitive listening, caring expression of feelings, needs, and requests. To communicate in this way builds resonance and trust between those who have been in conflict. To listen in this way means to seek to touch the soul, the long-lost innocence behind the eyes of the one before you, no matter how unconscious and destructive they have been before. Nonviolent Communication has been used to help groups in the conflicts from Rwanda and Kosovo to the Congo and Colombia.

It was in this spirit that I recently worked with activists and those engaged in conflict resolution in Burma. These brave monks and nuns, students and leaders, these were kindred spirits. We explored strategies to spread open-mindedness and truth, and drew on the ancient Buddhist principles of social harmony and wise society. But on the streets the military government was secretly stoking a growing fear and prejudice against Muslims. There was a huge anti-Muslim and anti-immigration campaign, with rallies, broadsheets, and social media trolls. Taxi drivers and merchants often spoke with scathing prejudice and racism about "them" and how dangerous "they" are. I have heard similar prejudice against Gypsies on the streets of St. Petersburg, against Arabs in Jerusalem, prejudice voiced in every country I have visited—in

Asia, Latin America, Africa, and of course North America. It is painful to see how much suffering grows from ignorance and a closed mind. Now, in response, the activists in Burma are spreading the teachings of lovingkindness and mutual respect instead of hate. They are countering fear and intolerance with love. And with the election of Aung San Suu Kyi, there is a growing shift in Burma and with it a hope that the scapegoating of Muslims will be reduced.

Open-minded listening allows you to know the perspectives of others. Whatever your view is, others look at the situation differently. Deep listening does not negate your own experience, feelings, needs, or preferences. Instead, it offers an air of mutual compassion in which problems can be seen and a multiplicity of perspectives understood. You can approach tough situations, whether religious and political, or tiny ones, like whose turn it is to take out the garbage, defensively, rigidly knowing how it should be. Or you can keep a beginner's "don't know" mind and see more clearly how the situation affects you and all those around you.

The world is bigger than it seems to a closed mind, it is bigger than your memory and opinions. Of course, you will have views and opinions. But it is the clinging to them that keeps you stuck. Lao Tzu notes that "the philosopher is wedded to his opponent." To be free, Ajahn Chah says, simply step out of the battle. Rest in the loving awareness that is your true home. While you can treasure your values, make room for others. This graciousness will serve you in all the inevitable changes of this mysterious world.

In any moment you can take a breath, open yourself beyond your preconceptions, see the world with beginner's mind. Feel how your body responds when you do, becoming present and at ease, relaxing into the openness. Notice when you are open, how others relax their own defensiveness. Let yourself be curious, loving, and concerned. Learn to see in new ways. It's never too late to open your heart and mind.

PRACTICE
Is This True?

With tenderness and respectful curiosity, take some minutes to ask yourself:

Whom do I look at with a closed mind? (Both individuals and groups.)

What do I look at with a closed mind?

How do I hold the world with a closed mind?

Now, take a person, a situation, or a perspective that you view with a closed mind.

Try reversing your perceptions:

Can I know that what I believe is absolutely true?

What if what I normally believe is not true?

Is there another way to see this?

What if the opposite is true?

How can you be sure it's not?

What is the suffering that comes from holding this view as fixed?

How does it feel to drop what you think and look again, fresh?

Chapter 10

The Gift of Authenticity

> *There is a vitality, a life force, an energy
> translated through you into action.
> Because there is only one of you in all
> time, this expression is unique. If you
> block it, it will never exist.*
>
> —MARTHA GRAHAM

People who don't put on airs, who aren't hiding behind a façade, are great to be with. They are just themselves—honest, straightforward, open. This kind of openness is your true wealth. Not imitating, nor striving to be like anyone else, being yourself in a full, honest way. Joyful or depressed, anxious or lonely, grateful or worried, honor it all: your gifts, your problems, your blemishes. It is so refreshing when a person speaks honestly.

You Were Born to Do This

In a letter to *Sun Magazine* in 2010, Erika Trafton describes this scene with her child:

> *"Am I gor-geous?" my child asks, drawing the word out like pulled taffy. "Yes," I say. "You are." The pink and teal dress is probably made of highly flammable material, some chemist's approximation of tulle and satin. Pudgy fingers decorated with pink polish trace the sequins on the bodice. "I love this!" A giant pair of bubble-gum-pink wings flap slowly. Little feet dance in sparkly red slippers. "I'm just like a real princess!" "Yes," I say, "you are."*
>
> *Curly hair, joyful smile, flawless skin. This child is the American epitome of beauty. This child, my son. He is four and a half years old and prefers to wear dresses. Maybe it's a phase, maybe not. Even as I wonder how I produced such an angelic-looking creature, I wish he would put on some pants and go back to playing with toy tractors—not because it matters to me (it doesn't) but because I am already hearing in my head the name-calling he will face in kindergarten. Many adults are already disturbed by the dresses. Strangers utter awkward apologies when they realize he's not female. This culture has no room for little boys who want to be gorgeous.*
>
> *He picks up a parasol a neighbor gave him and opens it jauntily over his shoulder. "Am I beautiful?" he asks. I sweep him into my arms and plant a kiss on his cheek. "Always."*

Though this story is told by writer Erika Trafton, it is our story as well. We are all both Erika and her son. Look in the eyes of a three-year-old. Every child has a spirit that is naturally free, that wants to dance, play, shout, and create. Over time, as our spirit is enculturated and disciplined, we can become shut down. Sometimes it seems as though our spirit is lost, but it isn't; it's just dormant. The child of the spirit in you is waiting for you to freely express himself or herself even now.

In a cartoon of a serene ocean bottom, two small fish are speaking to each other. One says, "I want the whole thing, the little glass bowl, the plastic castle, the blue pebbles." Some people buy sailboats because their spirit comes alive tacking into the wind. Others buy sailboats because all the neighbors at the club have boats and they think they should have one, too. Live your *own* life, not one of comparison. In Zen, it's expressed simply, "Don't draw another's bow; don't ride another's horse." No matter what the world around you wants, there is only one person you can be true to, and that is yourself.

Staying True

The modern world makes it difficult for us to know ourselves. The loss of connection with ourselves starts early, when we want to survive and be loved and included. We look around and imitate others; we try to figure out how to fit in. Often our family, school, and community don't value our unique spirit. They want us to act as we are "supposed to," not as we are.

One seven-year-old went out with his family and neighbors to a nearby restaurant for dinner. When the waitress came to take the orders, Josh said he wanted "a hot dog and root beer." His mother turned to the waitress and said, "He'll have the meat loaf, mashed potatoes, green beans, and milk." The waitress finished taking the rest of the orders. As she left the table, she turned back and asked, "Do you want ketchup or mustard on your hot dog?" As she disappeared, Josh joyfully piped up and said, "She thinks I'm real."

Too often our culture suppresses spirit rather than celebrates it. A front-page article in the *Wall Street Journal* reports that 45 million American children between the ages of two and twelve are on antidepressants, ADHD medication, and anti-anxiety, antihypertensives, and antipsychotic pills. Too often boys and girls who are too rambunctious and full of life to sit all day at their school desks are medicated, when they simply long to run around. And it's not just the children. In addition to widespread addiction to prescription drugs, modern adults constantly email, text, speed, consume, drink, and misuse other drugs to keep themselves busy, to take the edge off.

The garden door opens the moment we see the ways we are caught inside. Seeing ourselves clearly, unadorned, is the beginning of freedom.

To Whom Are You Faithful?

When do you feel most free to be yourself? There are a thousand possible answers: when I'm alone, at parties, when I'm traveling, after a couple of drinks, out in the woods, with my kids, working, cooking, riding my bike, sailing, watching football, with my girlfriends, on vacation. And when do you feel least free to be yourself? At the office, in social settings, with my in-laws, in front of a crowd. What does each situation feel like? When you work, do you feel free to be yourself—creative, stubborn, slow or speedy, collaborative or inner-directed? In your tasks and pleasures, how true do you feel to yourself? Are you living your own life? When you write or speak, is it an imitation or are you telling your own story? As you grow in mindfulness, you come to know yourself better, and your clarity will grow stronger. You will see your habits, your fears and conditioning. And alongside them you come to know your deeper feelings and values, your gifts, vision, and purpose. You are able to witness yourself with perspective and become more deeply alive.

A good friend and dedicated meditator, the CEO of a leading American corporation, came to a retreat at Spirit Rock. In the first days of his retreat, like most meditators, he saw his attention wander and body ache. He went over unfinished conversations, reruns of experiences and future plans. Gradually, as he settled in, his mind became quieter, his attention steadier, the qualities of peace and lovingkindness began to fill more of his sitting. We met each day, and he reported his changing experience and insights. He saw so much more clearly the patterns he had inherited, the problems he had to solve, the desires, the ever-changing insubstantiality of it all, the wisdom of letting go.

In our last private meeting, he was clear-eyed and grateful.

He smiled at me and said something unexpected: "I should have dressed better for this retreat." I asked why, and he answered, "When you're meeting yourself for the first time, you want to look good!" We laughed out loud together.

When you determine to be yourself, you realize there are many selves. At times, you can be an introvert or an extrovert, an anarchist or a Republican. You can be sick, then well. A soldier, a healer, a parent, and a fool. Your interests, tastes, understanding, values, circumstances, and even health change. Who you were long ago was you then. You change constantly. Yet underlying all these changes is a fundamental freedom, the treasure of being present, alive now. With this freedom, you can follow your deepest longings and stay true to the marrow of your bones.

Don't be afraid to stretch, explore, discard, try things out, let go, and experiment. There is creativity, contradictions, and splendor in being human. Walt Whitman has reminded many generations: "Do I contradict myself? Very well then, I contradict myself. I am large, I contain multitudes." As you become faithful to your own vast being and your silent inner nature, there comes a fullness and courage. As conditions and your outer expressions of yourself change, let yourself change, too. Celebrate all of who you are.

Start Where You Are

You are born with a unique temperament, personality, and capacities. You learn, grow, develop, struggle, suffer, triumph, forgive, hold on, and let go. Sometimes your life is easy, with health and prosperity. Sometimes it's tough, taking care of a disabled child or a sick parent, or struggling to find work or put food on the table. Even under easy circumstances, you might still feel unfulfilled or depressed, not knowing how to manifest your gifts or deepest intentions.

Remember the spirit of Nelson Mandela. Freedom starts exactly where you are. Honor this place, whether it is easy or difficult. Sometimes you are free to change circumstances, sometimes not. Andrea, who was taken to the hospital after a stroke, describes her long healing process. "Lying in the hospital on those dark nights, slowly relearning to move parts of my body, the practices of mindfulness and love have given me a way to move through the difficulty, finding blessings and joy, a kind of grace everywhere. How often we want our circumstances to be different, but this moment is it, this is our life. *Here* is where we can be free."

Even when you are immobilized—locked in prison or, as Stephen Jenkinson describes, when "a terminal diagnosis has come elbowing its way into your scheme for contentment"—inwardly you are still free. Wherever you are, remember that no one else can lead your unique life. You are the only author of your autobiography.

Chuang Tzu says, "True men and women of old weren't afraid when they stood alone in their views. They took life as it came and went their own way, without relying on others." You are free to decide how to live your life. In the end, you must.

Aware Inside, Calm Outside

Your feelings can help you find the way. In American culture, people are commonly taught to shut down their feelings. I notice this especially when I return to the United States after traveling to more demonstrative cultures such as Italy or India or Mexico, where love and affection, grief, anger, and celebration are more openly expressed. Sometimes I feel as though I've returned to a cultural refrigerator.

This cultural emotional guardedness mirrors the way that feelings were shut down in my own family. By the time I reached college, I was out of touch with my anger, grief, fear, and need. Being shut down limited my experience of love and joy as well. When the door of the heart closes in fear of painful feelings, beautiful ones get shut out, too. Practicing meditation as a young man, I finally began to recognize more of my feelings.

Buddhist psychology describes us as having a river of feelings. Mindfulness helps us begin to know and acknowledge what we feel. As a monk, I learned to notice and name them as they arose, resting in loving awareness. Now when I teach, I use an English list of five hundred feelings to help people recognize this river. It starts with A's such as accepting, addled, admiring, affectionate, aggressive, agonized, ambitious, ambivalent, amorous, amused, angry, anguished, antagonistic, antsy, anxious, apathetic, apoplectic, aversive, and B's like bad, belligerent, bewitched, blue, bonkers, bored, bouncy, brave, brokenhearted, buoyant, and ends with feelings like wary, whimsical, wild, wistful, wondrous, worried, zany, zealous, zestful, and zoned out.

Once we learn to recognize feelings, the next step is to feel them fully and finally, to express them appropriately.

Many people have difficulty feeling grief or anger, fear or shame. Some people have difficulty letting themselves feel happy or joyful. To feel what you are feeling, the first step is to identify and acknowledge each feeling as it arises. I sometimes ask students to keep a notebook logging all the feelings they notice in a day or a week. If you've been shut down, this can be difficult. It can help to inquire together, so with some students I will sit together as the person names whatever is present. If she says, "I'm feeling nothing," I note, "Nothing," and ask her to carefully describe what nothing actually feels like. She might slowly report quiet, empty, numb, tingling, bored, dull, open. These are subtle feelings and she has begun to recognize them in herself. Then I ask her to think of a beloved person and say out loud what feelings come. Then I ask her to picture the most difficult person or enemy and say aloud different feelings that arise. She might say afraid, angry, hurt, sad, or frustrated. This is the beginning of learning to acknowledge, differentiate, and tolerate feelings.

The next step in this process is to use loving awareness to experience them in your body. Is it felt as shaky or stiff? Pulsating or still? Warm or cool? How does it affect your heart? Your mind? Your breathing? Do you become tight or open, more agitated or calm, does it feel pleasant or unpleasant to experience this? How so? What other feelings accompany this one? In this way you can make your feeling life conscious.

Honoring Your Feelings

Jennica had been meditating for years when she learned her husband had had a long secret affair and hid much of their money. As he abruptly ended their marriage, he said many hurtful things. When she came to talk to me, I asked, "Have you considered revenge?" She broke out in nervous laughter. Of course she had, but a "spiritual" person isn't supposed to have thoughts like these. I described several forms of possible revenge, and we laughed a lot more. She was relieved. We weren't actually considering a vengeful response, simply acknowledging her powerful feelings.

After learning to acknowledge my feelings as a monk in Asia, I entered graduate school in psychology, where the next steps in my education in feelings came alive. I became involved in a tempestuous relationship with a woman I'd met in college, which in a short while triggered my old family pain. Insecurity, anger, desire, and dependence all came up. From my mindfulness training, I could recognize what I was thinking and feeling, but I was still unable to express strong emotions. I had learned to suppress intense feelings, to stuff them inside to maintain control, due to my childhood fear of the explosive anger and sorrow in my home. Now, studying the complement of Eastern and Western psychology, I entered therapy with Myron Sharif, a psychologist at Harvard Medical School, who had worked with the controversial and brilliant body-centered psychiatrist Wilhelm Reich.

Myron tried to help me express my feelings. I had become adept at being aware of what was going on inside while staying calm outside, which Myron called "the monk's defense." After a frustrating period when not much happened, Myron asked what time of day was most difficult for me. I said early morning. I don't function well at that time; I like to sleep late. Myron laughed and scheduled our sessions for 6:00 a.m., "when my ego defenses would be down." At six he would have me lie down and do powerful breathing practices to energize my whole system. Then he'd have me tell stories of my past. Sometimes he'd put on arias from great operas, and while I listened, charged up from the rapid breathing and filled with my stories, he'd push and manipulate my body to help free energy and emotions. He worked so vigorously that one morning he accidentally cracked two of my ribs.

It worked. Little by little, I became able to rage and weep and shake with fear and excitement. I became more fully aware of my feelings and less afraid to express them, freer to *choose* my response. Anger, aversion, and desire were no longer terrifying forces that needed to be bottled up; they became an energy of aliveness to feel, surrender to, or use as skillful means.

In the forty years since I left the monastery and worked with Myron, I've learned to be more at ease around strong feeling states, letting them be or, when called for, expressing them. Grief and tears, anger and strength, joy and sorrow move through me now in a more open and natural way, and I help others feel, express, laugh at, and honor their own feelings.

. . .

Like me, you may have learned to shut down your feelings, fearing you'll lose control or be overwhelmed. With the practice of loving mindfulness, you can gradually extend your window of tolerance for them. When you can name, acknowledge, and feel each feeling—allowing the heat of anger, the tears of shame, the heartbreak of grief, the delight of pleasure, the exuberance of joy—you'll discover that each has a story to tell, and under the stories are other feelings. As you find the courage to be with your own feelings, to honor each of them and let them inform your life, you will become more free.

The next step is the freedom to express your feelings. Not all at once, not dumping your anger or hurt or anxiety onto others, but expressing, "This is how I feel. This is what I most want. This is what I need. This is what matters to me." To fully connect with others includes bringing feelings as well as your intentions to the relationship. Doing this can be scary. If, as in my family, your childhood feelings were suppressed, any display of tears, anger, frustration, or needs can be terrifying. Your inner critic or judge will rise up, and your fears of being scolded, shamed, hit, or shunned might be overwhelming. If you come from a wildly expressive background, where rage, grief, frustration, demands, wants, and conflicts were flying around, you can also be terrified. In this case, you may be afraid that expressing your feelings will unleash destructive floods and overwhelm others. With mindfulness, little by little, you can learn to simply give voice to your feelings. It may feel awkward or even scary, but like all the other dimensions of being yourself, it will be amazingly liberating.

Desire

One of the most confusing feelings we experience is desire. Some people mistakenly think a spiritual life is one free of desire. But the human realm is a desire realm. As poet Alison Luterman explains, getting rid of desire is like hiding the chocolate chip cookies because you are on a diet. Meanwhile, you are the only person in the whole galaxy who knows where those cookies are hidden. Desire is part of us. Freedom and love require that you understand desire and see that you are free to choose which desires to follow. There are healthy desires that come from the depths of your being, from a healthy love of life. And there are unhealthy desires based on addictions, grasping, greed, fear, inadequacy, and imitation. Explore your desires, and if they are not harmful, try them out.

Pick a current desire in your life. It can be material, like a desire for a new smartphone or pair of shoes. It can be the desire for a friend's approval, a raise, or to lose weight. Bring it to mind and notice where and how you feel it in your body. Is it warm or cool, contracted or pleasant, tense or empty? Do you feel it in your stomach, your head, your heart? Is it always the same? What stories does it tell about fulfillment, about how satisfied you could be, about you, about the future? Notice what emotions come along with it, like need, longing, judgment, restlessness, fear, or frustration. Notice when you act on desire unconsciously, reflexively. Notice, too, what happens as you become the witness of desire, holding it with loving awareness. Does it shift, increase, disappear, hide? Notice if your desire is healthy or destructive.

With loving awareness, you can step outside of desire and, because you are not identified with it, become free to choose.

Deepen your study of desire. See how much desire runs the world—business, agriculture, politics, romance, and procreation. Notice how modern advertising and consumer culture promote a field of desire. They reinforce our wanting, our unexamined sense of longing and incompleteness, the illusory feeling that we are separate and not whole. Observing them closely, we can notice that wanting and desires are fleeting, without essence, but when we are caught by wanting, it is like an intoxicant, and we can't see clearly.

Do not confuse desire with pleasure. Pleasure is a natural and blessed part of our human experience. The problem with the wanting in desire is its grasping, as if grasping one desire after another will create a happy life. But desire is endless. Learn to know the limitations of desire and choose wisely. George Bernard Shaw said, "There are two great disappointments in life. Not getting what you want and getting it."

My Indian guru, Nisargadatta, explained, "The trouble with you is not that you desire, but that you do not desire enough." He went on, "You limit yourself to desires for certain wants, needs, hopes, and ideas. Why not desire it all? Discover that you are everything and nothing, then your desires will be fulfilled." Honor desire with loving awareness and let it connect you with all life.

Free to Be Human

Much attention is given in public forums to outer freedoms—and these are critically important—freedom of speech and religion, freedom from oppression, economic freedom, freedom for girls and women to learn, to create, and live their lives equal to those of men. These are hard-won and precious freedoms, and regularly we are called upon to defend them courageously and expand them. To do so is both a necessity and an honor. Outer freedoms are a treasure. And standing up for them is one of the greatest acts a human being can do.

With all the cultural focus on outer freedom, we seldom reflect on the freedom to live fully, to be awake and alive to ourselves, to know our own mind and heart and the sound of our own song. Yet we treasure those who do. In modern times, we can look to Georgia O'Keeffe, who left New York to paint in the wilds of New Mexico; to Paul Gauguin, who left Paris to paint in the South Seas; to Einstein's visionary equations; to Steve Jobs, Albert Schweitzer, Amelia Earhart, and Eva Péron.

Rumi suggests we dedicate ourselves to a large, foolish project as Noah did. If you could make your life over, even now, what would you do? How would you live more fully, true to yourself? How would you be self-possessed in a healthy way? How would you live with more integrity, inside and out? Be responsive to life? Be your quirky, splendid, eccentric, honest, tender, and courageous, creative self?

Why not do it? Go out and dance, plant, write a poem, dedicate yourself, change jobs, sit in silence, speak up, make money, have a baby, plant a garden, start a movement, move to paradise, move back to your hometown. You are freer than you think!

PRACTICE
Being True

Take some time to sit, quiet your mind, and listen to yourself deeply. Reflect on these questions: How does it feel when I am most true to myself? What are the circumstances and times that foster this? How can I bring this to more of my life? Make space for any answer. Your true nature may be to accommodate and collaborate with others. Or it may be to go it more alone.

Now ask, where am I least true to myself? What are the circumstances and times that foster this? How does this feel? What do I envision would be the result if I was more true to myself?

Without trying to change others, simply out of respect for yourself, what do you believe might happen? Keep an open mind.

Most important, can you envision being true to yourself and expressing yourself with love? How would it change your life to live this way?

Chapter 11

Free to Dream

All human beings are also Dream Beings.
Dreaming ties all mankind together.

—JACK KEROUAC

Creativity makes us happy. When we look around at the modern world, every bridge and building, every garden and shirt, the spoon and table in front of you, your pasta and salad dressing and its recipe all began as a creative thought in someone's mind. We live in a sea of creativity made visible. Take a moment and open to this enormous force. The natural world is endlessly creative, clouds and waves and plants of every form, a million species of beetles, new mountains always pushing up across the globe, unique sunsets every day. We human beings, as part of this natural process, also create, moment by moment, century after century. Picture the people who envisioned weaving the first threads of linen or cotton, who made the first glass windows, who designed the first cart, who created drinks from cocoa beans, who for thousands of years experimented with makeup and tattoos. This is your lineage.

Express Your Heart

When you see life as an opportunity to bring your creative spirit alive, you are free to contribute joyfully and fully. The measure of suffering you experience, the struggles of your life can all become the materials of your creative palette. Whether you do it consciously or not, you can transform the grit of your life into art. Sometimes through poems or paintings, sometimes through tending a hidden garden or eking out a living in your unique way. Wherever you find yourself, let your circumstances awaken the creative freedom in you. No matter what the situation, give the world a spirited response.

After the tragedy of 9/11, a professor at a Manhattan art college described how despondent his colleagues had become. Many felt that in the face of such devastation, making art seemed frivolous, unnecessary, absurd. His response:

> I couldn't answer any more than I could have answered if they had been arguing the redundancy of beauty, or breathing. What could I say? That in June 1945, workers reclaiming the Nazi prison camps found poems, folded in thick squares, stuffed up into the electrical wiring . . . that a person awaiting interrogation or death would

choose to hide a poem on a piece of toilet paper so that their spirit facing death could not be taken from them.

Whatever your circumstances, you are free to pen your poem, dance your dance, express the depths of your own heart.

"Bird Got My Wings"

I have seen creative freedom expressed by men in San Quentin prison-dharma programs. Jarvis Masters lives on death row and has undertaken the Buddhist practice of nonharming. He tells the story of being in the prison yard one winter day when a seagull landed in a puddle of water. A big young inmate next to him picked up a rock to throw at the gull. Following his vow of compassion, Jarvis instinctively raised his arm to stop the stone thrower. The young inmate shouted angrily, "What you think you're doin'?" Everyone in the yard, even the guards, got quiet and alert to see what was going to go down. You ordinarily don't mess with another person's private space in prison, or you do so at your peril.

Jarvis turned back and spontaneously blurted out, "That bird got my wings!" Hearing this, the young man peered at Jarvis quizzically, trying to understand, and then gradually lowered his stone. His face softened. Everyone relaxed. No one quite understood. But they all relaxed. For days afterward, Jarvis recounts, inmates on the cell blocks would come up to him and ask what he meant by "That bird got my wings." It was like a Zen koan. Jarvis never answered, he only smiled. And yet, instinctively, everyone knew what he was talking about. Even when your body is confined in the prison yard by razor wire and guard towers, there is a freedom. Your spirit can fly free like the gull lifting its wings over San Francisco Bay.

Maybe this is a good thing to do when you are in trouble. Say something a little crazy.

While your situation may not be as dire as for those in San Quentin or as dramatic as the 9/11 attack in New York, in the midst of your own life, your spirit is free. Outwardly, you might be limited by the culture you live in or the insistence of time, by the personalities of people nearby, by your aging body, the necessities of your finances, or the hovering of death over your shoulder. Yet, like Jarvis and Nelson Mandela, you have a part of you that is free to respond creatively—no matter what.

They're Your Dreams

Art professor Howard Ikemoto recounts, "When my daughter was seven, she asked me one day what I did at work. I told her I teach people how to draw. She stared back at me, incredulous, and said, 'You mean they forget?'"

Perhaps you remember when your elementary school art teachers didn't recognize the masterful giraffe you had just drawn or complained that the sky you drew (like Van Gogh) wasn't supposed to be orange or yellow or pink. Maybe the chorus director in music class told you to mouth the words because you couldn't carry a tune. Maybe you stopped singing or painting or dancing or planning your flight to Mars decades ago. You despaired because they said your life wasn't creative in the right way.

Don't let others' ideas deceive you. Don't let despair deceive you. Step outside of old ways of thinking and use the materials of your own life. *Imagination* is creativity's first step. A visitor to a French stone masonry asked several of the workers what they were doing. The first said he was cutting and leveling the face of a stone block. The second said, more brightly, that he was cutting stone to make a good living. The third responded joyfully that he was helping build a great cathedral.

The creative spirit is not bound by fixed hours or certain jobs. It cannot be lost. Simply open the inner gate. For a thousand generations your ancestors have sung songs, painted images, danced, drummed, built and designed and cooked and decorated and prayed and traveled. Just as it is in the nature of coyotes to howl, the wind to blow, maple leaves to turn red and orange, children to twirl and dance and laugh, it is in your DNA to create.

Everyone is an artist. Sometimes it bursts forth, sometimes it waits underground. In retreats, together with mythologist Michael Meade and poet Luis Rodriguez, I have taught young men from juvenile halls and vets returning from our Afghan and Iraq wars to turn their suffering and survival into art. Powerful rituals, truth telling, and revolutionary poetry release the creative voice in these men. Many had never written a poem or a story, some had hardly read anything longer than a few sentences. But when they heard Luis's heartrending poems and felt the encouragement of the group to express themselves, each found he had a powerful story to tell, a betrayed or stifled cry that became a compelling tale or poem, a voice that needed to be heard.

To be creative is not frivolous or trivial or optional. It is your lifeblood moving again, your tongue honoring this intimate and strange adventure, your making a visible mark on the mysterious trail of evolution. You are reclaiming your soul.

Crafting Your Life

You may think, I'm not an artist or even a creative person. But you *are*, and the canvas is your life. Your life *is* your creation, whether wild or small, whether limited to a chair in the corner of a room or to a hospital bed, whether traveling to Timbuktu, having a fabulous family, or six generations of family dysfunction.

When you understand that your life is your canvas, your dreams can open and become bigger or more modest, more playful, genuine, tender, caring, or intense. Here are some questions for you: What is the vision of your life? What limits your imagination? What is your style? What kind of art do you want to make?

When you look at the arc of your life, you can recognize your family's history and society's expectations. These are important to see clearly and honor, but they are only the start, not the end. They merely set up the canvas. Acknowledge your circumstances, then step back and let your vistas open. Do not look at your life as something forced upon you, but see it as the screenwriter and director, and dream where the plot will go from here. Recognize that outer circumstances—fate and destiny—can propel a dream:

the racism that inspired Gandhi, the horrors of the Crimean War that motivated Florence Nightingale, Monet painting in his glorious garden, the training in calligraphy and travels in India that sparked the vision of Steve Jobs. Let your circumstances invite your dreams.

Every life is a visionary journey, a creative palette. Yours may start as a shopkeeper, a small business owner, a contractor, yoga teacher, accountant, single mom, computer science teacher, or wedding planner. Wherever you are, step back and reflect. What is the most beautiful vision you have for your life's canvas, starting just where you are? More of the same, but sweeter and deeper? Or do you envision a change of home or occupation? Further education? Travel? A quieter, more contemplative, inward-focused life or greater social engagement? A new art or new style or new love? A willingness to set off in an unknown, uncharted direction?

As you imagine the possibilities, notice how your doubts, limitations, and reservations also arise. You fear you don't have the energy, the time, the freedom, or the money. You have to fulfill your responsibilities to family, work, community, friends. You just couldn't. It would shake up the family, disappoint too many people, put your established scene at risk.

These are the voices that can stop you from growing. Feel their grip. Let them have their say, acknowledge, and bow to them. Notice that they are only thoughts. Then ask yourself, "If I could do anything, what would it be? How would my life change?" What would be the first steps to move into this new creation of my life?

Will you regret not having given it a try?

Conscious and True

To create art, you need to wed discipline and letting go. Saxophonist and jazz composer Charlie Parker explains, "You've got to learn your instrument. Then, you practice, practice, practice. And then, when you finally get up there on the bandstand, forget all that and just wail."

To create a killer app, write a new song or computer program, work for social justice, plant a garden, or build a business requires discipline. You need to endure repetition and keep going. To widen your creative channel, open the gates and become trusting, willing to fail, fall, get up, work, play, practice, repeat, and learn. The Stoic philosopher Epictetus says, "If you wish to be a writer, write." Playwright Paddy Chayefsky explains further, "Artists don't talk about art. Artists talk about work. If I have anything to say to young writers, it's stop thinking of writing as art. Think of it as work. . . . Art is for academics. Art is for scholars. Art is for audiences. Art is not for artists."

Bring style to whatever you do. I have seen immigrant workers cleaning bathrooms and tending ailing patients with the radiant smiles of saints. I have seen kids' basketball coaches combine loving and fierce discipline with such a generous heart that everyone around them rose to their best.

Let the canvas of your life have style! Tattooed or country club, nonprofit or Wall Street, collective or solitary, introverted or wildly social—play with your style, dream it, experiment, enjoy it. You can dream a big dream and start a cable news network like Ted Turner did or dream an exquisite small one like a Persian miniature, delicate as a daffodil or steady as a giant sequoia. You *are* the canvas. Create something conscious and true.

The most engaging people are those interested in life. Creativity comes alive with interest, and interest is always specific. For the astronomer, it's the shape of this galaxy; for the designer, the slight round curve of the tool in the palm; for the cook, the aged English cheddar and just-crushed garlic and fresh, green garden mint leaves; for the poet, it is noting the uneven lift of an eyebrow and the cacophony of crows on a high-tension wire over the dilapidated inner-city soccer field. As you become present, interested, attentive, and mindful, your freedom and creativity grow.

The Currents of Life

Let the creative process start to move through you. Pick a discipline, pay attention to the masters in your field. Practice your craft, your art, your dance, your skills. Then open to a bigger, more mysterious flow. Creativity needs letting go, an attentive releasing to allow something new to be born. Follow your instincts, your feelings, your senses, your body. Let a small feeling of irritation become a rivulet that leads to a poem whose rush of feeling breaks through a dike holding back anger with God and at the extinction of the rhinoceros. Let a jiggling foot or a tense shoulder make a movement that grows into dance and ecstatic release. Let a restaurant's tympanic sounds in your ear become a spontaneous rhythm, the music of the world, like that of John Cage's Experiment. Initiate wildly, break up, build up, try deliberate errors, circle, get down, get over your ideas, get over yourself, and above all, trust. Creativity is a way of allowing the ever-renewing energies of life to move through you.

I was writing a book in the pristine quiet of the San Anselmo Theological Library when a gardener began using a loud leaf blower right outside the window. I was annoyed; I wanted it to stay quiet. After becoming mindful of my frustration and releasing it, my mind relaxed and I was ready to write again. But I couldn't. To my surprise, I couldn't hear the words. I realized then that that is how my creativity works: I hear the words and write them down.

The next week at a charity dinner with other well-known authors, I shared this story to see if they also hear the words and then write them down. Two said yes. Another writer said she sees images and writes to describe what she's seeing. Another said his writing comes up from the earth through his body and out through his fingers. Your creative energy has its own channels for revelation and expression.

When you open yourself to creativity, faith in life's wellspring grows. This trust allows you to listen, collaborate, fail, discover, explore, and see anew. As you open and listen, something new will be born. Rilke explains, "Being an artist means ripening like a tree which . . . stands confidently in the storm of winter not afraid that summer may not come. It always comes."

Dream Big and Dance

Kittens and puppies roll and run around, otters and chimps tease and chase each other, children who don't know whether they are rich or poor all play, simply to engage the world, to be alive. French film icon Jeanne Moreau, being interviewed, said, "I shall die very young." "How young?" she was asked. "I don't know . . . maybe seventy, maybe eighty, maybe ninety. But I shall be very young."

Whatever brings you alive is the channel for your freedom. Delight in creativity for its own sake. Grow and nourish your dedication and expression and care. Whether your vocation or vacation, your occupation or avocation, free the creative spirit to dance with you.

A new father told this story:

I am an artist. When my daughter was born, and I was there at the hospital, I remember talking with the doctor about what I did for a living. The doctor confided in me and said, "I wish I had been a musician, because I love to play the concert piano."

Later, after my wife had the delivery, the doctor came out with the good news that my wife was now fine and I had a brand-new healthy baby girl. While we're standing there and I was receiving the good news, another doctor walked up to the physician who had just completed the cesarean surgery that delivered my child and said, "Excuse me, doctor, I just wanted to tell you that you performed brilliantly in there, it was an honor to assist you."

I turned to the doctor and said, "Now tell the truth. You have just brought a new life into the world, saved another life, and you've had one of your colleagues tell you it's an honor to be in your presence—for heaven's sake, can you honestly say you wish you had been a musician?"

The doctor grinned, nodded his head, and said, "It went pretty well in there." We both chuckled and then the doctor said, "I know exactly why, too—because this morning, I got up early and, for one hour, I played Chopin at the piano."

What wants to be danced, expressed as art? Try something new. Draw left-handed. Write a poem. Learn to tango. Paint your truck. Start a creative project and connect with others. Give away your tomatoes and zucchini on the street corner. You are not just here to toil. Dream big and dance.

PRACTICE

You Are an Artist

Take twenty to thirty minutes to step back from your workplace, your desk, your computer, your sink, your easel, your garden.

Go for a little walk. Look at the subtle colors of the sky, the shimmer on the thousand forms of leaves around you. Listen to the myriad sounds around you and add to your walk a favorite piece of music from your phone. Sense that you are in the movie of your life. You are actor, director, and writer. See your roles, the parts you have taken for this section of the story. Smile. Some of your part is already written and cast, but how you play it and how you rewrite new scenes is up to you.

Find somewhere to sit quietly. Reflect on your life as a work of art, with its loves and triumphs, its tragedy and comedy, its losses and redemption.

Envision that you can add more artistry to your life. This might be literal, and you will see yourself creating an app, making videos, painting, dancing, surfing, writing poems, practicing Aikido, growing prize-winning roses.

Now envision your whole life as a work of art. What can you do to add more artistry to your life? Like Shakespeare, in your own time you will have to live amid comedy and tragedy, leadership, love and conflict, loss and reconciliation. What sense of style, what playfulness could you add? What would make it more poetic, more heroic, more tender, and more beautiful?

No one has lived this ever before. It is yours to play.

Part Four

Living Freedom

Follow the grain in your own wood.

—REV. HOWARD THURMAN

Chapter 12

Deliver Your Gifts

Trust that little voice in your head that says,
"Wouldn't it be interesting if . . ." and then do it!"

—DUANE MICHALS

Puanani Burgess writes, "[What] if we were able to see the gift in each of our children and taught around that gift? What would happen if our community was gift-based? If we could really understand what the gift of each of our communities were, and really began to support that?" You can engage life as a co-creative part of the world. You are free to walk out the door or lock yourself in, sell everything, make a fuss, make music, make love, turn toward or run away, invest, build, write, explore, sleep, or go to Las Vegas. Freedom is an urgent, beautiful, large responsibility and natural consequence of being human. Each of us has our unique gifts and expression. We're here to deliver our gifts.

Free to Act

Knowing you are free to act can liberate you from inner constraints. But you also need to understand that you are not free from consequences. If you break the law, you can end up in jail. If you betray another, you can ruin a relationship for life. Nevertheless, you *are* free to act, experiment, learn, explore, err, express yourself, hide, and begin again. It's your game.

Sometimes we don't feel free to act. We feel nervous, reluctant, discouraged, or enervated, even paralyzed. Or we feel overwhelmed by the world and its never-ending cycles of poverty, conflict, and injustice. Politicians and media feed our fears, and fear sways voters and sells papers. Don't buy it! Yes, there are big problems—climate change, war, racism, economic exploitation. If you only worry, you'll feel overwhelmed. What is indisputable is that you are here, now, and you *can* contribute. Edward Everett Hale explained, "I am only one, but I am one. I cannot do everything, but I can do something. I will not let what I cannot do stop what I can do." You are free to contribute to this world—every moment, every day.

Try Again

But what if I make a mistake? you might think. What if I fail? When Krishnamurti told Vimala Thakar, his reluctant disciple, to begin to teach, his instruction was, "Don't be afraid to fail." Mistakes are necessary. They are the natural scientific method—

experiments by toddlers repeatedly testing gravity; in the same way you learn to surf, write, speak, ride a bicycle, make music, and make love. Buckminster Fuller said, "There are a number of very important irreversible truths to be discovered in our universe. One of them is that every time you make an experiment you learn more: quite literally, you cannot learn less."

Sometimes we're frightened to act because we are afraid of how we will look. Notice what it feels like to act when it's about "you," your worth, self-consciousness, self-esteem, image. Sometimes to compensate we act grandiosely, trying to show we are better than we believe deep down. It can be an interesting experiment to reflect, "What if this action that makes me nervous is not an assessment of ME? What if it is just a creative experiment, one in a thousand acts to try out and see what happens?" Yes, of course you will still care somewhat how it looks. But if your spirit is playful, honest, relaxed as well as committed, not about ego but true to your self, those around you will feel this.

Freedom to act is immediate, imaginative, spontaneous, and refreshing. Beauty arises when the freedom to act is wedded to stillness. Find ways you can quiet yourself so that you can sense in your heart what really matters. From there you can plunge into the world from a place of authenticity and function at your best. As you quiet your mind and open to the reality of the present, you will know what to do. Sometimes your action will be to create a new school or company or garden or novel. Sometimes you'll act to stop oppression, harm, or injustice. Sometimes your best action is nonaction, offering an attentive, caring presence.

This can all be done with love. Gandhi would step out of his role as leader and take one day each week in silence, to listen and clarify his deepest loving intentions. Acting from his highest truth, he inspired millions. The best revolutions that have swept the world have carried a new vision and transformation that had been unthinkable before. A revolutionary spirit is ours to bring alive.

Even war can be reenvisioned. Gandhi's close friend Khan Abdul Ghaffar Khan organized the greatest Peace Army the modern world had ever seen. In the 1930s in Afghanistan and Pakistan, then called the Northwest Frontier Province of India, he trained more than one hundred thousand devout Muslims, and they vowed to resist British rule nonviolently with their lives—all without weapons or hatred. They kept their vow and succeeded despite massive provocation and many attacks on them.

Acting freely springs from stillness; it is strengthened by inner listening. Even so, your course of action might not be clear. It might be mixed with confusion, habit, or superficial desires. You can expect there to be setbacks. Don't worry. Sometimes you simply need to try, to take one step and see where it leads.

Vision and Action

Jacques Verduin started the Insight Prison Project at San Quentin, which has spread to other prisons. Its purpose is to offer mindfulness and compassion teachings as support to the huge number of men and women incarcerated in America's terrible prison system. He spoke to the warden at San Quentin about starting an ongoing program for men who wanted to turn their lives around through anger management, forgiveness, and mindfulness practices. With perseverance and a lot of paperwork, he was granted a space in the chapel to offer a regular class. Arriving at the first session somewhat excited, he was surprised and disappointed to see that only one man from the prison had chosen to attend. A well-respected elder, Ali, a practicing Muslim, introduced himself. He had come because he wanted to find out what Jacques was intending to teach. Jacques began to talk to him about the value of developing the spiritual strength of mindfulness and inner training. Jacques felt awkward teaching a class for one inmate.

So, Jacques asked Ali about his Muslim practice and heard about the diet, the ethics, and need for regular prayer five times a day. Then Jacques said simply, "Would you teach me how to pray?" Carefully removing a prayer cloth from his pocket and showing Jacques the direction to Mecca, the inmate anointed the insides of Jacques's wrists and the back of his neck with perfumed oil and taught him to bow. After a period of silent prayer together, they arose and sat quietly for a minute. Then the older man laughed and said, "You're okay. I'll tell the guys to come down here for your class." The next week the chapel was filled with interested men, and the ongoing program is now statewide.

Inner stillness helps you know how to respond. Take time to be alone, walking in nature, contemplating, listening to music or birdsong, or just being still. You can nurture this inner connection every day. Even in micro-moments, you can check in. When you stop at a red light, relax your shoulders, feel your breath, listen so the next action you make comes from what is most free and authentic in you. When you are true to yourself, you inspire others to do the same. William Butler Yeats explains, "We can make our minds so like still water that beings gather around us so that they may see their own images and so live with a clearer, perhaps even a fiercer life because of our quiet."

Vision is fulfilled by action, and action must be informed by vision. Together, wisdom is born.

Bring Your Gift

Hawaiian educator Puanani Burgess tells this story:

One of the processes I use to help people talk to each other I call Building the Beloved Community. There's an exercise that requires people to tell three stories.

The first is the story of all of your names. The second is the story of your community. The third story I ask them to tell is the story of your gift.

One time, I did this process with a group in our local high school. We went around the circle and we got to this young man, and he told the story of his names well and the story of his community well, but when it came time to tell the story of his gift, he asked, "What, Miss? What kind gift you think I get, eh? I stay in this special ed class and I get a hard time read and I cannot do that math. And why you make me shame for, ask me that kind question? What kind gift you have? If I had gift, you think I be here?"

This boy just shut down and shut up, and I felt really shamed. In all the time I have ever done that, I have never, never shamed anybody before.

Two weeks later, I am in our local grocery store, and I see him down one of those aisles and I see his back and I'm going down there with my cart and I think. "Nope I'm not going there." So, I start to back up as fast as I can and I'm trying to run away from him. And then he turns around and he sees me, and he throws his arms open, and he says, "Aunty! I have been thinking about you, you know. Two weeks I have been thinking: 'What my gift? What my gift?'"

I say, "Okay, bruddah, so what's your gift?"

He says, "You know, I've been thinking, thinking, thinking. I cannot do that math stuff and I cannot read so good, but, Aunty, when I stay in the ocean, I can call the fish, and the fish he come, every time. Every time I can put food on my family table. Every time. And sometimes when I stay in the ocean and the Shark he come, and he look at me and I look at him and I tell him, 'Uncle, I not going take plenty fish. I just going to take one, two fish, just for my family. All the rest I leave for you.' And so the Shark he say, 'Oh, you cool, brother.' And I tell the Shark, 'Uncle, you cool.' And the Shark, he go his way and I go my way."

And I look at this boy and I know what a genius he is, and I mean, certifiable. But in our society, the way schools are run, he is rubbish. He is totally destroyed, not appreciated at all. So, when I talked to his teacher and the principal of the school, I asked them what would his life have been like if this curriculum were gift-based? If we were able to see the gift in each of our children and taught around that gift? What would happen if our community were gift-based? If we could really understand what the gift of each of our communities were, and really began to support that?

So that for me is a very native approach—being able to see the giftedness in every aspect of life.

The whole purpose of human incarnation, says Malidoma Somé, an African shaman and friend, is to bring your gift into the world. Among his Dagara people, they say each person is born with a certain cargo to deliver to this earth. Nothing else creates so much fulfillment and meaning in life as expressing your unique capacities and offering your gifts. Like with this boy, your family, culture, or education might not recognize your gifts. It is up to you to know and value them, to deliver your cargo. Pay attention to what you love. What lights you up. What do you care about? See if you are drawn to flying, surfing, gardening, science, politics, sports, music, community organizing. Try them out, make a fool of yourself. Be orthogonal, fresh, brash, or do the obvious. Be inspired by this young man's epiphany, honoring his gift of fishing, providing food for his family.

Angie Thieriot and Patricia Phelan began to work together in 1978 out of concern for how dehumanizing and cold hospitals had become. Together they started Planetree, a health-care organization that has become a global leader in patient care. When you go into a hospital, as a patient or family member, or even a part of the staff, it is obvious how the benefits of the technological systems, the twenty-four-hour monitoring and speed and impersonality, can also be very difficult for patients, making it hard to sleep and hard to get well. Angie and Patricia decided to create an alternative. A Planetree model hospital unit does not feel, look, or sound like a hospital. Classical music plays softly in the background. Patients wear their own robes and pajamas, sleep on flowered sheets, and are encouraged to sleep in as long as they like. There is no nurses' station. Instead there's a study area where patients are encouraged to read their own charts and write in them as well. There are no official visiting hours: friends and family are welcome at all times convenient for the patient. Family members cook for their ailing loved ones in a patient's kitchen. Interested family members are trained to serve as active care partners. At Planetree, things are arranged for the convenience of the patient. As their director notes, "Once patients get a taste of the Planetree model, they simply won't permit themselves to be admitted anywhere else."

Selfless Service

You are free to change the world around you. In the *Bhagavad Gita,* helping others, selfless service, is called a direct path to God. At first, your serving might feel only partly selfless. Don't worry. Even good works can begin with mixed motivation. You might begin because it looks good or you're supposed to or from guilt or because you want something back. It doesn't matter. As you serve, gradually you will discover that helping is like caring for your own child, your own body. You don't say "Awww, I guess I have to help my left ankle" if it is injured. It is a part of you, and you naturally respond with care. "The trouble," said Mother Teresa, "is that you draw your family circle too small." Everyone is your aunty or uncle, niece or nephew, and when they need help, you need help, too.

Sometimes you will embody active service. Michael Meade, group leader and mythologist, is also a drummer. He created a traditional drumming community for a large group of lost boys of Sudan who were airlifted to Seattle for safety. These young men had run away from rebel military attacks that destroyed their villages and killed their families. They spent months barefoot in the desert surviving lions and marauding soldiers. They were adrift in their new home in Seattle, so Michael got them drums and helped create city-wide healing and welcoming rituals for the lost boys.

Everyone has the capacity to be a healer to other people. Sometimes the most important help you can offer is your loving presence. Laura, a neonatal nurse, makes it her practice to care for the sickest, tiniest babies, the ones kept alive with needles and probes, holding each baby with her hands, her fingers, her breath. Huston Smith, the great professor of world religions, tells of his enormous grief when his granddaughter was killed. "Many people responded kindly," said Huston. "But the most helpful of all was my young Native American neighbor, who came over every day and just sat next to me silently."

As you share what you love, you become free in entirely new ways. The Iroquois nations had a ritual to teach this to their young children. Making a large tribal circle, they would feed a small child full and then outside the circle a voice would call plaintively, "I'm hungry, I'm hungry." The child who had just experienced abundance would be encouraged to follow his natural impulse and take food to the hungry one. Then the ritual would be repeated with warm deer skins and woven blankets, and when the young child was toasty and warm, he would hear "I'm cold, I'm cold," from outside the circle. And the child would take some blankets to whoever was cold.

The myth in America is one of independence—the settler and the cowboy who do everything for themselves. But those individuals, too, were held, fed, and cared for as babies; they were taught and educated. All their tools and trade and medicine came from others. As independent as you feel, you are also interdependent.

As you grow in freedom, you sense this interdependence. Then you realize you are not helping any one, it's us: our body, our family, our planet. What do you want to give? What is your gift waiting to be brought forth? What would it take to free this gift?

The World Needs You

It is easy to feel overwhelmed by global problems. Climate change. Children fleeing violence in Central America. Wars across the Middle East. Streams of refugees. Racism. Prison reform. Black Lives Matter. Homelessness. Economic injustice. Political gridlock.

These are part of the fabric of the human race at this time. But the solutions to these problems are also within you. I remember talking with my mother about the problems facing humanity in this era. She reminded me that she was born when her father came back from World War I. She had lived through worse times than those of the twenty-first century, the Great Depression, World War II. She reminded me that humanity survived even these terrors. We have eventually found ways to respond, to renew.

Now our task is to renew yet again. It is obvious that there is no outer solution. No amount of new technology, computers and internet, space technology, nanotechnology, biotechnology will stop continuing warfare and racism and environmental destruction. This is a pivotal point in our history. The powers of science and technology now must be matched by the inner developments of humanity. The chairman of the Joint Chiefs of Staff called us a nation of nuclear giants and ethical infants. But this is not the end of the story. We have learned that empathy, integrity, and wisdom can also develop. The research of Harvard professor Stephen Pinker, detailed in his book *The Better Angels of Our Nature*, shows how, in fits and starts, global violence has actually decreased in the last few centuries. And with it, slavery has been reduced. The rights of women and children are becoming gradually better than they were a hundred years ago. The rights of gays and lesbians, of refugees and the disabled have grown. Not everywhere, for there are still too many people enslaved, threatened, or living in dire poverty. But collectively we must resist backsliding and honor that we are headed in the right direction.

Humanity must go much further. It is possible. We need an educational system based on compassion and mutual understanding, and a profound sense of interconnection. We need mindfulness and mutual care to guide our communities, our medicine, our politics. We need a new way to approach our problems.

My colleague Wes Nisker interviewed Pulitzer Prize winner Gary Snyder. At eighty-four, Gary is one of our greatest poets and environmentalists, and he has been writing about the environment for more than fifty years. Wes asked him about the climate problems, global warming, rising oceans, loss of species. Did Gary have any advice for us? "Don't feel guilty," he said. "Guilt and anger and fear are part of the problem. If you want to save the world, save it because you love it!"

The problems of the world need your love. Love is the only power great enough to overcome greed and anger, violence, and fear. This is the love that has mothers lift cars off their children. Martin Luther King Jr. called on the nation to embody the power of love. As you gain a greater sense of inner freedom, you become available to the world in a new way. Not as a frustrated, frightened, or burned-out activist. But with an inner strength. The inner freedoms you discover— freedom to love, to create, to awaken, to forgive, to dream, to start over—all naturally give rise to a greater care for life.

In Zen, they say there are only two things: You sit, and you sweep the garden. And it doesn't matter how big the garden is. As you quiet your mind and listen to your heart, you discover that your spirit will not be satisfied unless you also tend your garden. Pick something you care about. It can be local or global, reducing racism or fighting climate change. Educate yourself, make close friends of others who are different from you, join the local school board, volunteer at the hospital, work for a political cause, or help the school plant a garden. Lower your carbon footprint. Add your voice and energy. Plant seeds for a more compassionate future. You can't change it all, but your freedom empowers you to contribute to the world, and your love gives you the way to do so.

Your Very Flesh Shall Be a Poem

You don't have to start big. William James wrote, "I am done with great things and big plans, great institutions and big success. I am for those tiny, invisible, loving, human forces that work from individual to individual, creeping through the crannies of the world like so many rootlets, oozing water, which, if given time, will rend the hardest monuments of pride." Start with the smallest gesture.

The Associated Press reported a donation to the earthquake relief fund for the people of Haiti in 2010. It spilled out of an envelope—$14.64 in crumpled bills and coins, from the pockets of folks at a Baltimore homeless shelter with a simple message: "We are worried about our homeless brothers and sisters in Haiti."

Wangari Maathai started planting a few trees, and by the time she was given the Nobel Prize, her group had planted 50 million trees. Mother Teresa began by picking up one sick and destitute man from the streets. A little at a time. Step by step you can open, even tentatively.

Find new gestures to enhance the palette of your own life. Celie retired from her job as an accounts manager, moved to live in the country, and became an integral part of an organic cooperative in her county. You might buy a sailboat and then, like my brother, teach sailing to the disabled. You might tutor immigrants, coach soccer, run for office, travel to Mexico, tell your kids you're sorry, live a life that you will never regret.

When you dare to act and stay true to yourself, your freedom will empower those around you. The *Tao Te Ching* explains, "When you are true to yourself, you are true to the Tao. You remind those around you of who they have always been." Hindus call this life a cosmic dance, the *lila*. Dance your own unique dance. Don't worry about how you are supposed to look and don't hold back.

When you act with authenticity, even if it appears to serve others, it is also for you. When Gandhi was asked what motivated him to sacrifice and do so much for India, he smiled in response and explained, "I don't do it for India, I do it for myself." Paradoxically, when you act true to yourself without being caught in aggression and fear, as you serve yourself, you serve and inspire others. Like the bee that collects honey and pollinates the flowers of the world, harming none (although if endangered, able to sting), move through the world bestowing blessings.

Walt Whitman encourages freedom in this way:

This is what you shall do: Love the earth and sun and the animals, despise riches, give alms to everyone that asks, stand up for the stupid and crazy, devote your income and labor to others, hate tyrants, argue not concerning God, have patience and indulgence toward the people, take off your hat to nothing known or unknown, or to any man or number of men—go freely with the powerful and with uneducated persons, with the young, and with the mothers of families—re-examine all you have been told in school or church or in any book, and dismiss whatever insults your own soul; and your very flesh shall be a great poem.

PRACTICE
Deliver Your Gifts

Sit quietly for a time, allow your body to settle and your mind to quiet. You, like all humans, have strengths, gifts, capacities that you bring to this world. Honor the fact that you are unique and idiosyncratic and one of a kind. Like the boy who can call the fish, or the native youth who sat quietly with a grieving grand-father, you have your own gifts. Let these questions resonate:

What brings you most alive?

What do you love to share?

What makes you feel most creative?

When do you feel most connected to yourself?

When do you feel most connected to others?

What concern on this earth do you most want to change?

What do you like to work with?

What do you like to play with?

What do you enjoy?

What brings you the most ease?

What do others appreciate about you?

What are your passions?

What have been your most blessed times?

Do you love:

>*Stillness? Tending? Organizing? Moving? Connecting? Social jus-*
>*tice? Planting? Solitude? Building? Healing? Listening? Lead-*
>*ing? Finance? Cooking? Feeding? Dancing? Figuring? Sports?*
>*Engineering? Experimenting? Traveling? Art? Children?*
>*If you were to list three strengths, what would they be?*
>*How can you develop and express these gifts?*

Chapter 13

Freedom in Challenging Times

Only when people made up their minds
that they wanted to be free, and took
action, was there a change.

—ROSA PARKS

In each human life there is praise and blame, gain and loss, success and failure, pleasure and pain, light and darkness. Has anyone among us not experienced all these? Each has its role, including the difficulties, and as the poet says, "Gradually darkness can school your eyes and your heart to find the luminous spirit, the true gifts that are required to navigate, hidden in this night's corner."

Our Challenge

Every generation or so, modern society is rocked by upheavals, whether by assassinations, war, political turmoil, or powerful economic and environmental challenges. In uncertain times the political leadership can worsen these fears. As H. L. Mencken reminded us, we are often deliberately encouraged to be afraid. It is natural to feel angry or frightened. When upheavals happen, we worry for our future or for the fate of the vulnerable around us. We may fear a rise in inequality, racism, environmental destruction, homophobia, sexism, or myriad other injustices.

But these very challenges are the opportunities humanity has to face to grow. As Ralph Waldo Emerson noted, "Only to the degree that people are unsettled is there any hope for them."

To find freedom amid challenging times, we have to start with ourselves. How do we manage our own bodies? If our limbic system is activated into fight, flight, or freeze mode, we lose our selves in survival fears. The reptilian brain takes charge. Tidal waves of worries swamp our thoughts about what lies ahead. In difficult times, these tides of angst and fear can flow back and forth between one group and another. We wonder, are things getting worse or are they simply getting uncovered? And how can we respond?

Stop. Tune in to your heart. That is where love, wisdom, grace, and compassion reside. With loving attention, feel what matters most to you. Yes, there are anxious thoughts, and there is grief and trauma, but don't let your heart be colonized by fear. Take time to quiet the mind and tend to the heart. Go out and look at the sky. Breathe in and open yourself to the vastness of space. Sense the seasons turning, the rise and fall of dynasties and eras.

Breathe out and dwell in loving awareness. Practice equanimity and steadiness. Learn from the trees. Become the still point in the center of it all.

Thich Nhat Hanh reminds us that in uncertain times, our own steadiness can become a sanctuary for others. "When the crowded Vietnamese refugee boats met with storms or pirates, if everyone panicked, all would be lost. But if even one person on the boat remained calm and centered, it was enough. It showed the way for everyone to survive."

Two thousand years ago, Rabbi Tarfon said, "Don't be daunted by the enormity of the world's grief. Live justly, love mercy, and walk humbly. You are not expected to complete the work, but neither are you free to abandon it." Clarissa Pinkola Estes continues this thread: "Ours is not the task of fixing the entire world all at once, but of stretching to mend the part that is within our reach."

Together, let us tie our shoes and walk in the direction of truth.

Listen with Your Heart

How then do we respond when we are surrounded by fear or anger? Loving awareness invites deep listening to all that is, including fear and pain. Father Thomas Merton points the way: "Of what use is it to travel to the moon if we cannot cross the abyss that separates us from ourselves, and from one another?"

First, turn toward yourself. Listen to the fears that are rising up. Be present for whatever is in your heart, listening deeply to yourself. Hold with tender compassion all that arises. Then, when you are ready, listen in the same way to others.

My beloved wife, Trudy Goodman, meditation teacher, colleague, and inspiration to me, has been working in the Darfur refugee camps on the border inside Chad, in Africa. She joined an inspiring project called iAct, run by friends of her Insight LA community. From the start, iAct was wise. They went to the camps and simply asked the women what they wanted. Aid workers often come in with an agenda, but iAct went in and just listened. The women they found there said they wanted two things. They wanted soccer, so their kids would have something uplifting to do and would learn to cooperate with one another. And they wanted a preschool and kindergarten, so that these little, often traumatized kids would begin to learn about themselves and the world. Because Trudy had run a school for children with difficulties, she was able to help train the teachers there in mindfulness, healthy child development, and the arts of emotional intelligence.

It's beautiful to ask people what they need, and then listen deeply. From this, mindful, wise action, beneficial action, can arise.

Vinoba Bhave was probably the most important follower of Gandhi. After the violent partitioning of India and Pakistan and the assassination of Gandhi, Vinoba went on retreat. When a couple of years had passed, Gandhi's followers organized a great conference to continue his work, and they asked Vinoba to lead them. He declined. They persisted, and finally he said, "I'll come under one condition. I need to walk there."

The walk took six months across a big swath of India. As he walked, he'd go into each village and sit with people under the big tree that is the gathering point for many Indian communities. Creating a listening circle, he'd ask, "What is your life like? What's happening for you as human beings?" And he'd hear how the poorest among them, the Untouchables, were for all intents and purposes indentured. They were farming someone else's land for a pittance, and they couldn't make enough money to raise and feed their children.

Vinoba became progressively more troubled, and one morning he called a group of villagers together and told them, "When I return to Delhi, I'll meet with Prime Minister Nehru and get the government to give parcels of land to the landless so you can grow your own food." The community was delighted, but as Vinoba went to sleep that night, he was shaken. He realized that by the time the government money wound its way in a lengthy bureaucratic process through the hands of the state, provincial, and district leaders, there wouldn't be much left for the poor.

So the next day Vinoba called another meeting. He apologized and expressed his concern that his plan would not work. He was not sure what to do next. After he explained the problem, a wealthy landowner stood up and said, "You have come here carrying the spirit of our beloved Gandhi. How much land do you need?" There were sixteen landless families, and each needed five acres to farm. So the man said, "In honor of Gandhi-ji, I will grant eighty acres to these families." It was a beautiful gesture.

Vinoba continued walking to the next village, listening to the villagers' concerns, especially the problems faced by the Untouchables, the outcasts. Then he told the story of what had happened in the village before. Inspired by this, another wealthy elder stood up and offered five acres for each poor, landless family. This became the start of what Vinoba called the Bhoodan Indian Land Reform Movement. Vinoba walked to the conference collecting two thousand acres of land. Then joined by others he continued walking for more than a decade. He walked through every state and province in India, and inspired landowners, who voluntarily turned over 14 million acres of land to those who had nothing. It was the biggest peaceful land transfer in the history of the world, all done because he sat under the trees and listened to what people needed.

It is not just people who need to be heard. When my daughter was in third grade, she gave me a sheet of paper written in her elementary-school handwriting. "Daddy, I think you can use this for your teaching." It was a famous passage from Chief Seattle: "What is man without the beasts? If all the beasts were gone, men would surely die from great loneliness of spirit. For whatever happens to the beasts, also happens to man."

Listening means listening to life, listening to the beasts, to the earth, so that we can respond in a way that is direct and courageous and intelligent. No matter what.

Join the Web of Care

My twin brother has a rare blood cancer and is in the middle of a difficult treatment program. For months, I've been visiting hospitals and cancer centers with him, and I've witnessed profound, devoted, loving care by doctors, nurses, and staff. Sometimes they succeed; sometimes they don't; but their care is invariably beautiful. I've sat next to families of patients of every age—brothers and sisters, moms and children. There is something so tender about it.

Sitting there, I feel all the people in the world who are tending to someone sick. Letting myself see and feel this worldwide web of care is profound. Amid illness and difficulty, the care and love people offer one another is magnificent. It is everywhere.

Look into the eyes of another person, even a glimpse. It doesn't have to be a soulful, doe-eyed stare. Just glance at someone near you. This being is going through a life journey with its joys and struggles, as you are, as we all do. And underneath it all they, too, seek to be well, happy, and loved.

As you quiet yourself and tune in to another being, you start to feel a natural care. George Washington Carver instructs us to open this care: "How far you go in life depends on your being tender with the young, compassionate with the aged, sympathetic with the striving, and tolerant of the weak and strong. Because someday in your life you will have been all of these."

Do not exile anyone, the disenfranchised, the hurt, the angry, the arrogant, the helpless.

All it takes is a little attention, and a natural wish for another's well-being arises from your heart center: "I wish her well. I pray that he has friendship, love, and compassion for his difficulties. I hope she is free from struggle, happy, and peaceful." Care is innate in us; it just needs attention. As you quiet your mind and listen, as you drop into your heart, you connect to the essence of things. And adding your care to the world is the magic that changes everything.

Blessed Unrest

Entrepreneur Paul Hawken spent a decade studying organizations that work for human well-being and environmental justice. From billion-dollar nonprofits to one-person, backyard endeavors, he discovered millions of individuals and groups doing important work. These people collectively comprise a massive movement with no name, leader, or location. As in nature, this organism is evolving from the bottom up as an extraordinary, creative expression of needs and solutions. Hawken's book *Blessed Unrest* explores the brilliance of this movement, its innovative strategies and hidden breakthroughs. These neighbors and friends, support groups and teachers offer a million acts of goodness. We are the ones we have been waiting for, and we are enough to inspire all who despair. Humanity's collective genius surrounds us. At the most difficult time, the glass may look empty, but these forces of brilliance and kindness remind us to reimagine a future we can celebrate.

In 2016, His Holiness the Dalai Lama and Archbishop Desmond Tutu, old friends and both in their eighties, spent a week together in a dialogue about happiness. They were asked how they can laugh and remain hopeful in spite of the difficulties in the world. This was a deeply personal question. Tutu lived through the horrors of apartheid, years of oppression, when people all around him were shot and killed for the color of their skin. The Dalai Lama continues to listen to the terrible stories of Tibetans who were imprisoned and tortured and who walk, some barefoot, over the Himalayas to see him. Yet these two elders carry a sense of joy, even in the midst of sorrow.

What makes them happy are the practices of gratitude, forgiveness, generosity, humor, and compassion. Most of all, it is the caring for others that keeps them grateful. No matter what the circumstance, being able to serve and help beings in trouble brings the highest satisfaction and the deepest form of happiness.

The Dalai Lama and Archbishop Tutu also keep a playful perspective. Discussing death and dying, the Dalai Lama says to Tutu, "I suppose you're going to go to Heaven."

The archbishop responds, "And you?"

His Holiness replies, "Hmm. Maybe, Hell."

Tutu says, "I thought Buddhists believe in rebirth," and after a pause, adds, "I hear the Chinese government is picking your next birth, so you better treat them well!" They laugh together and continue to tease each other.

After one rambunctious exchange, Archbishop Tutu admonishes the Dalai Lama in mock seriousness, "Look here—the cameras are on you, stop behaving like a naughty schoolboy. Try to behave like a holy man." Then they laugh some more.

No matter what the subject, they exude a deep celebration of the life they've been given and demonstrate the beauty and magnificence of life, as it is.

When asked about his own rebirth, the Dalai Lama will often say it is uncertain. My teacher Ajahn Chah used to say the same thing. When people would ask him the big questions, he would just laugh and say, "It's uncertain, isn't it?"

"How can we be sure what are the best teachings? What should I do with my life?"

"It's uncertain, isn't it?"

"What about enlightenment."

"It's uncertain, too, isn't it?"

"You're supposed to be enlightened."

"That's uncertain, too, isn't it?"

This is called the wisdom of uncertainty. To become wise, you must become comfortable with not knowing.

In uncertain times, we must care and respond, but we cannot know the time frame for the fruit of our actions. Gandhi explains, "You have to do the right thing. You may never know what results come from your action. But if you do nothing, there will be no result."

Stand up for justice, mend the divisions, heal the wounded, tend the vulnerable, celebrate human possibility. Plant seeds for the long term. And trust Dr. Martin Luther King's vision from the mountaintop: "The moral arc of the universe may be long, but it bends towards justice."

And know that amid it all, there is another kind of certainty. When my daughter was small, I took her to Yosemite Valley. She reached down, picked up a colored rock, and was in awe. "Isn't it pretty, Daddy?" She didn't need to look up at the spectacular waterfalls and 3,000-foot cliffs; to her, everything was Yosemite.

We can certainly have that same sense of wonder and delight—no matter what.

Lead with Humanity

"O, nobly born," begin the Buddhist texts, "remember your Buddha Nature. Remember the fundamental Dignity that was born into you." You can hear this dignity in this story told by Lenore Pimental in *Sun Magazine*.

The man was my age but looked many years older. He was an army veteran. He was also homeless, cold, and hungry. I could see he tried to wash up before coming to the social services department to ask for help. His face and hands were clean, but his clothes were filthy. Though he claimed not to have had any alcohol that day, the smell of it seeped from his pores. I wanted to get him into rehab, and I asked if he was ready to come in off the streets. "No, ma'am," he said. "All I'd like is a few dollars and some bus tickets. If I can get sober enough, they'll let me into the shelter across town." That shelter had fifty beds, cots really. The homeless were admitted at night and forced out at dawn to eat breakfast at a nearby charity. Fifty beds and nearly a thousand homeless in this part of the city.

Winters here in Northern California mean cold, rain, and mud. Even though this man and many like him slept under bridges to keep dry, the dampness penetrated everything. His clothes and the bedroll he placed on the floor smelled moldy. The pages of a book he carried were swollen. I asked him how many times he tried rehab. "Two or three," he said. "A long time ago." "Maybe it's time to try again." I explained that I'd had a client who'd gone through the program seven times before it took. "Besides," I said, "we're months away from warmer weather. What else have you got going on?"

I watched his face as he considered my offer. I thought I saw a flicker of hope in his eyes. Followed by a shadow of doubt. He'd tried before. It had been hard, impossibly hard, so he was living on the streets. Finally, he lifted his head and looked at me. I reached for the phone. "Shall I?" I asked. He barely nodded, yes. An hour later I handed him over to a recovering alcoholic, also a veteran, who would drive him to one of the best rehab facilities in the county. "Come visit me when you graduate," I said as they left. I barely recognized the man when he came into my office six months later, so tall and handsome, smelling like the outdoors, and holding a huge bouquet of flowers.

This is possible. It's in us. There is something beautiful waiting to be touched in all those around us.

Be prepared to respond, but not to react. Reacting is natural, but a deeper strength grows from our ability to listen carefully to what is needed, even amid uncertainty. With humility, we can acknowledge what we don't know yet. We don't know what will happen politically. We don't know what will happen in the world. We have to look for possibility and listen deeply.

The *Tao Te Ching* asks, "Can you be still and not act until the right action comes of itself?" Can you let the mind and heart settle like stirred-up water until things are clear and you know how to act in concert with the Tao? It takes a kind of trust in the mystery, trust in the cycles of history. And then we can lead with love.

When Archbishop Tutu and the Dalai Lama were asked, "What do you do in times of despair?" they said, "You show your humanity."

Strategic and Strong

We are in the midst of something vaster than any current social and political dynamics. We are in the midst of the evolution of humanity. And we each have a role to play in this.

An ancient understanding says that human beings are the makeweights of the world. In traditional times, goods were weighed by a balance scale with two pans. On one pan the object to be weighed was placed. On the other a series of metal weights was placed. The most beautiful sets of weights were in the shape of animals like turtles and rabbits. The world is like this balance scale holding birth and death, joy and sorrow, good and evil. And in our time we humans are the makeweights, the last small weights placed on the scale. Depending on which side we place our actions, we will tip the scales.

Like the Tao, let yourself be still until the moment for right action. Be strategic. Make yourself a zone of peace. With the courage to be true to your heart, then you can act.

Remember, change always starts with a small number of people. In 1787, Thomas Clarkson and eleven other men started a thirty-year campaign that finally forced the English parliament to outlaw slavery. In 1848, Elizabeth Cady Stanton and four other women met in upstate New York to begin the seventy-year suffrage movement that led to women's right to vote. When you are strong in yourself you can act with courage, dedication, and directness. When you become strategic, you join with others, you choose the most important problems, and bring the most creative solution.

You know what is needed. The most powerful nation on earth must foster a vision of peace and cooperation, not spread weapons of war. The richest nation on earth must provide health care for its children, its families. The most productive nation on earth must combine trade with justice, sustainable development, and protection for the environment.

You can contribute. You have your heart, your voice, and your spirit. Be strategic and strong. Remember how Barbara Wiedner started Grandmothers for Peace. Sometimes it takes only a little loving awareness at the right moment. You can do it.

You know the right direction.

"Others will be cruel," said the Buddha. "We will not be cruel. Thus we will incline our hearts.

"Others will kill or harm living beings. We will not harm living beings. Thus we will incline our hearts.

"Others will be greedy. We will be generous. Thus we will incline our hearts.

"Others will speak falsely or maliciously. We will speak truthfully and kindly. Thus we will incline our hearts.

"Others will be envious. We will not be envious. Thus we will incline our hearts.

"Others will be arrogant. We will be humble. Thus we will incline our hearts.

"Others will be unmindful. We will establish mindful presence. Thus we will incline our hearts.

"Others will lack wisdom and kindness. We will cultivate wisdom and kindness. Thus we will incline our hearts."

Your presence is an expression of the wisdom you carry. Through your steadiness, compassion, and deep values, you become a bodhisattva—a being dedicated to compassion no matter what. You can stand up for the environment, for immigrants, for whatever is in front of you that needs your care and attention. People are hungry, you feed them. Someone is hurt, you bring whatever healing you can. You stand with the poor and the vulnerable.

You do this not because you're supposed to, or because you are a special person, but because, as the Dalai Lama says, "the only thing that brings joy in this life is service."

Do not just shake your head and frown when you read the news. Do not be fooled into believing that you cannot change things. As Thomas Jefferson says, "One person with courage is a majority." You can make a difference.

And remember, a person with courage never needs weapons, but he or she may need bail.

Trudy told me that the greeting in the Darfur refugee camps is "How is your family?" It turns out that your family is all of humanity, all the animals, all beings on earth. Your family includes Greens, Libertarians, Democrats, Republicans, and all the in-betweens. Include them all in your heart.

Live with gratitude. The times ask for a change of consciousness—a shift from the fearful, separate consciousness, the consciousness of us versus them, to the consciousness of connection and interdependence. You are already part of this shift. Now each of you, in your way, is invited to find a freedom of spirit no matter what happens, and to carry what's beautiful into the troubled world.

When Leonard Cohen so movingly sings of how it all went wrong, the song on his lips still sings Hallelujah.

Remember his gravelly voice and his love.

Keep your heart strong.

Carry what's beautiful within you out into the world.

You Have Been Training for This

In the last years of the Obama presidency, I was invited to speak at the first-ever White House Buddhist Leadership Gathering. More than a hundred leaders from Buddhist communities across America came together and described how their inner practices were wed to a community commitment to the well-being of all. Their practices included care for the environment, tending of refugees, prison projects, care for the homeless, international peace work, food for the hungry, interfaith bridge building, support for vulnerable women and children, and projects to fight discrimination and support justice for all members of the society.

In my closing summary at the White House, I explained that the Buddha had counseled kings and ministers, and he had guided leaders of the society around him with teachings of peace and respect. Here is one record of his teachings to leaders that I read there:

> *As long as a community holds regular and frequent assemblies,*
> *meeting in harmony and mutual respect,*
> *can they be expected to prosper and not decline.*
> *As long as a community acts with wisdom and respect,*
> *can they be expected to prosper and not decline.*
> *As long as a community protects the vulnerable among them,*
> *can they be expected to prosper and not decline.*
> *As long as a community cares for the sacred places of the natural world,*
> *can they be expected to prosper and not decline.*

—FROM THE BUDDHA'S FINAL TEACHINGS

These wise teachings are found in other traditions. But what is most powerful about these Buddhist teachings is that they are taught together with practices that show us how to cultivate and embody them. As human beings we can actually train ourselves in compassion, mindfulness, respect for others, empathy, and inner balance. Modern neuroscience has reaffirmed that when training in compassion, social and emotional learning, wise attention, and self-regulation are included in childhood education, health care, and business, they benefit the individuals as well as those around them. The quality of academic work, health, productivity, and care for one another all increase. Compassion, mindfulness, and mutual respect are the basis for creating a wise society.

Spiritual practice is not a passive affair. The Buddha intervened to try to stop wars. He tried to broker peace in families and communities. He offered economic council to a king whose society was experiencing lawlessness and civil disorder. Instead of increasing taxes and suppressing the disorder by force, the king was encouraged to supply seed, capital, and support to farmers and businesspeople. The king was encouraged to promote fair wages for the community. As prosperity grew, the countryside became secure. He went on, "Secure people will sit with children in their laps and live with open doors."

The Buddha taught that greed, hatred, and ignorance are the causes of suffering. He showed ways to develop their opposites: love, clarity, wisdom, truthfulness, generosity, and gratitude.

In modern times, Buddhist leaders have done the same. Maha Ghosananda of Cambodia joined the United Nations peace process and led years of peace walks through the war zones and killing fields of Cambodia. Thai abbots have taken their robes and ordained trees as elders of the forest to protect ecosystems from logging. Burmese monks and nuns marched in the streets to protect citizens from the harsh military dictatorship. A. T. Ariyaratne in Sri Lanka enlisted hundreds of thousands in a 500-year peace plan. Vietnamese, Chinese, and Tibetan monastics have stood up for peace, justice, and compassion, some even immolating themselves to stop the harmful actions of governments.

Gandhi explains, "Those who say spirituality has nothing to

do with politics do not know what spirituality really means." This is not partisan. It is standing up for basic human principles—moral action and the prevention of harm. It is the embodiment of loving awareness amid the troubles of the world.

Whatever your perspective, now is the time to stand up for what matters—to stand against hatred, for respect, for protection of the vulnerable, and for the natural world. Meditation and contemplation, in themselves, are not the fulfillment of the path of freedom.

Loving awareness is *relational,* built on generosity, virtue, and lovingkindness. The path to human happiness and liberation requires intentions that are free from greed, hatred, and cruelty; speech that is true and helpful, neither harsh nor vain, slanderous nor abusive; and actions that are free from causing harm, killing, stealing, or sexual exploitation.

You are never alone in your care. Generations of ancestors stand at your back. You have the blessings of interdependence and community. You have the beasts of the forest as steadfast allies. You have the turning of the seasons and the renewal of life as the music accompanying your dance of life. You have the vast sky of emptiness holding all things graciously. With peacefulness and mutual respect, you and your communities can become centers of vision and protection.

You have been training for this moment for a long time, perhaps lifetimes. You have learned to quiet your mind and open your heart. You have learned about love and interdependence. Now is the time to step forward, the time to bring your equanimity and courage, wisdom and compassion to the world. Be the bodhisattva, the being of peace, who seeks to alleviate suffering in the midst of every imaginable chaos. When storms of fear and uncertainty arise, it is time—individually and collectively—to stand up, calm and clear, and with peacefulness and unwavering mutual respect become a center of vision and protection.

Protection takes many forms. It can be providing sanctuary for those in danger. It can be skillfully confronting those whose actions would harm the vulnerable among us. It can be standing up for the environment. It can be becoming an active ally for those targeted by hate and prejudice. Protection means carrying the lamp of loving awareness. It means standing up for the truth—no matter what.

Remember these timeless teachings: hatred never ceases by hatred, but by love alone is healed. Generosity, love, and wisdom bring happiness. Practice them. Embody them. Plant seeds of goodness, and well-being for all will grow.

A time of change has come. We must listen deeply, bear witness, honor everyone, and choose our actions wisely and courageously. Don't worry if the right action is not yet clear to you. Wait in the unknowing with mindfulness and a clear heart, and soon the right time will come and you will know to stand up.

I will meet you there.

PRACTICE

Stand Up

Try this simple reflection:

Imagine you could look back over this next year when you are at the end of your life.

And imagine, among all the demands of your life, that you had chosen to stand up for one cause, something you truly care about.

It might be global or local. Climate change, hunger, refugees, children, justice, or whatever matters to you.

And imagine how you feel at the end of your days having done so, having placed this makeweight on the scale of the earth.

Now imagine the first step, what you envisioned, who you contacted, how you began.

Finally, imagine how you can begin in the weeks ahead.

Now, carry your blessings and act.

Chapter 14

Live in Mystery

God made everything out of nothing, but the
nothing shows through.

—PAUL VALÉRY

The mystery is not far away. A child can hold a single acorn in which a thousand future oak forests rest. In each of the acorn's cells is a wildly twisted DNA chain that holds the history of deciduous trees and their evolution from the first forms of life. Look closely at the palm of your own hand and you can see the remnants of primate life and the future of humanity.

On this blue-green earth, our plants miraculously turn light into sugar. Your gut hosts 100 trillion nonhuman microbes, collaborating with your own cells to keep you fed without your direction. Meanwhile, your three-pound, complex brain, engaged just now to decipher these words, has quintillions of neural firing patterns, more than the number of stars in the known universe.

Look into the eyes of another. Where does this human incarnation come from? What will happen tomorrow? What is consciousness? Gravity? Love? Death? We live amid mystery all the time.

Not Far Away

Our capacities for knowing are, first and foremost, a mystery. We rely on our senses, our thinking, and perceptions. But there are many ways of knowing beyond these.

Lynne Twist describes visiting Senegalese women of a desperate and drought-stricken community who dreamed of exactly where to find water under the blazing Sahara Desert. It took a year of dusty digging surrounded by drums and songs until the water gushed free. How did they know?

When Elizabeth Mayer, a Berkeley scientist, was pressed by her mother to call an Arkansas dowser to find a stolen and valuable harp, he pinpointed it to a single block in Oakland. She found the harp there and turned her initial scientific skepticism into her book *Extraordinary Knowing*.

Our interconnection spans space and time. I read that the odds are that your next breath will contain at least one molecule of Julius Caesar's dying breath are 99 percent. Dubious at first, I calculated using Avogadro's number of 10 to the 23rd molecules per mole and the 10 to the 22nd number of liters in our atmosphere. It's true. You breathe with Julius Caesar.

The mystery brought me from an Ivy League college to a remote Thai-Lao forest monastery. When I ordained as a shaven-headed monk, gathering food with an alms bowl, it all felt familiar, as if I had done it many times before. Later, in deep meditation I had memories of being a poor monk centuries before in China. Who knows? It could be true. I used to think science explained everything. But it doesn't explain consciousness or birth or death.

Still, when I met Ajahn Chah in 1967, I told him I didn't believe in past or future lives. I explained that I came from a family of scientists. He laughed and said, "No need to believe. Birth and death happen in every moment. Pay attention to this and you'll learn everything you need to know about suffering and freedom from suffering." In the fifty years since then, I have changed. I didn't used to believe in anything. Now, after a lifetime of experiences, I pretty much believe in everything.

The Mystery of Incarnation

I could tell a hundred stories. My youngest brother's beloved wife, Esta, was weak, in the last stages of cancer, and I got up early to go see her. I had spent many days with her and knew her time was near. I sped down the highway and rushed through a brief errand at the drugstore on the way. As I stood to pay the cashier, my body softened and all the hurry disappeared. I knew she had died. Back in my car, I called my brother Kenneth, and he confirmed, yes, Esta had died peacefully a few minutes earlier.

In a similar way, a friend practicing in Burma had a vision of the accidental death of his father. He contacted home and, sadly, his father had died just as he had seen. You have all heard stories like these. They are true. Consciousness is not limited to your body.

My first out-of-body experience was during a yearlong silent retreat at a rigorous training monastery. I was instructed to sit and walk in meditation eighteen hours a day. An ardent young man, I threw myself into it. One day my body felt exhausted, so I lay on the hardwood floor of my *kuti* (hut) to take a brief nap. After twenty minutes, I got up and began a slow walking meditation to the far side of the room. I looked out the window at the other monks in the distant garden. When I turned around, someone was lying on my floor at the other end of the *kuti*. Shocked, I saw it was my own exhausted body. My spirit had been determined to get up despite the exhaustion. When I walked very close to my body, I peered down, fell into it, and woke up on the floor. Later I regularly experienced being out of my body and so much more—dissolving my body into light, entering the silent void, bliss, and unbounded love—lessons that opened me to seeing how eternity, freedom, and perfection always exist here and now.

After years of sitting with the dying, many of whom describe going in and out of the light as they hover near death, I've come to trust the reality of consciousness beyond the body. When I witness the mysterious and sacred moment of their consciousness leaving the body, I see that what is left behind is only the shell of flesh. I have remembered other past lives in my own meditation. And using deep meditations, I have led past-life regressions for people in countries around the world. Surprisingly, whether they believe in reincarnation or not, many remember being in families, villages, and farms in cultures past, and they see and learn from these past-life images. And when they let themselves reexperience how they died, they, too, feel spirit leaving their bodies, entering realms of light and luminous darkness until there arises the pull to enter a womb again. There is no need for you to believe any of this. Simply keep an open mind.

Who are you? How did you get into a strange human body with eyeballs, hip sockets, and nipples, with patches of fur in a few places and a hole at the upper end into which you regularly stuff dead plants and animals, grind them up, and glug them down through a tube? Where your ambulation is made by tipping in one direction, catching yourself, and falling in the other direction, and you create copies of yourself by inserting or receiving a tube that squirts a hundred million microscopic gooey tadpoles. Take a close look at your vestigial tailbone and the fingernails that are remnants of ancestral claws. Incarnation is wild.

Here is a powerful yet simple way to understand. Look in the mirror. You will see that your body has aged. But oddly, you will also experience that you don't necessarily feel older. This is because your body exists in time. It starts small, grows up, ages, and dies. But the consciousness that is looking at your body is outside of time. It is spirit that takes birth, experiences your life, and will witness your death, maybe even saying at the end, "Wow! That was an amazing ride!" Who you are is loving awareness witnessing the dance of birth and death.

Deep down you know this is true. In *The Color Purple,* Alice

Walker describes it this way: "One day when I was sittin' there like a motherless child (which I was), it come to me that feeling of bein' a part of everything, not separate at all: I knew that if I cut a tree, my arm would bleed. And I laughed and cried and I run all around the house. I just knew what it was. In fact, when it happen, you can't miss it."

The Earth Is Breathing You

You are consciousness incarnated in a human body, but not limited by it. Consciousness is the clear space of knowing, as vast as the open sky. Rest in consciousness, in loving awareness. Let vastness be your home.

Sometimes you remember vastness by grace. You go dancing and become the music, or you walk in the mountains or peer into the eyes of your beloved, and time and space dissolve into eternity. You lie on the bow of a sailboat, dissolving into the spray, or you open into vastness in meditation. When you're deeply attentive, if you look carefully you can see through the veil of separation. You can recognize the ephemeral nature of your personality, the habits of the small self, and recognize that when you feel yourself as separate, your mind is walled off, your understanding is incomplete. The small self feels separate, insecure, unfulfilled, and frightened by the ever-changing river of life. But deeper attention shows that you *are* life, you are the river, and your ever-present awareness can never be lost.

You are the consciousness witnessing it all, the loving awareness and the mystery from which it is born. Take a few deep breaths. Now let your breath return to its natural rhythm. Feel how life is breathing you, perennially inviting you into freedom and eternity, here and now. Even these words of freedom and mystery, like staring at a menu, can never satisfy your deepest hunger. Instead, feel this miraculous breath, this moment's pulse of life. As our former American poet laureate W. S. Merwin tells us, breath breathes us, rowing us across the river of our own life.

It is profoundly refreshing to step beyond yourself. Start by letting life unfold naturally, slow down, relax.

Doris was fifty and had three teenagers and a budding design career, but she was plagued with anxiety. "I was a worrywart, full of indecision and panic, and when I learned about mindfulness, it made so much sense. So, I went for a retreat. The silence and peace were blissful, no decisions to make, only to be present and kind to myself. What came first was a subtle change in the perception of who I am. I practiced a gentle acceptance of aspects of myself that I'd rejected and now felt grateful to know. I realized my heart had atrophied, and I held a lot of fear and pain inside, which prevented me from giving love to myself or others. This gentle opening left me less caught in suffering. I began to trust myself being fallible and human and yet so much more. Then what I call 'the miracle' happened. I was on a slow, mindful walk, totally quiet, and then I disappeared. There was no me, only vast silence and the wind. It was an hour of joyful and amazing freedom. Now I know that I am so much bigger than my fears. Some days I can still feel the vast dance, and others, I'm still standing on the sidelines. But all I have to do is unfold my arms and step forward into life, and I am free again."

You don't have to be afraid to open. When you let go of the usual sense of self, you are perfectly safe. Your body and personality and intelligence are still here. They become like your pets—you can feed and care for them and even enjoy their quirky qualities, but they are not "you." They are your wardrobe. Your free spirit is beyond them all.

Beyond History and Self

When you define yourself by your history and self-image, you can become really lost. You believe the stories you tell about yourself, about your body, your family, your history with its traumas and dramas, your failures and accomplishments. It is possible to step beyond your history. Reality is bigger than this. You are more than the stories, thoughts, and fears of the small self. Family, nationality, race, education, orientation—none of these fully defines you. They can be honored, but you are not bound by them.

Society likes to put us in boxes, but we are not stereotypes. There is no white person, no yellow person, no black, red, or brown person, no gay or straight person. We are unique individuals with dreams and idiosyncrasies whose lives are so much bigger than they might look to others. Over a lifetime, you are called upon to play many parts, but you don't have to identify with them. You can play your part with a mythic style as a warrior or a ne'er-do-well, you can act the part of a goddess or of an eternal adolescent, a great mother, a prince, a slave, or a servant of the divine. You can make your life story one of inner riches or poverty, sin and struggle, or joy and redemption. You can play victim or companion, workhorse or sage, nurturer, lost soul, loner, artist, or adventurer. Neuroplasticity can even rewire your brain.

Take a step back. Acknowledge your common roles and styles. Enjoy them—even the tough and sad ones. Get some perspective and humor. You are not these roles. You are beyond them. Even your body with its pleasure and pain, aging and illness, does not limit you. A person with physical disabilities is not defined by his body, nor by aging or illness or pain. I can still hear the voice of a quadriplegic man at a spiritual seminar exclaiming, "I am not my body. Hallelujah!" Anne Morrow Lindbergh observed, "The spirit lays the body on the altar." Your spirit is greater than the ever-changing forms of body and mind.

Interbeing: You Are Not Alone

When I teach, I carry with me a picture of Vedran Smailovic, a cellist from the Yugoslav National Symphony playing amid the ruins of Sarajevo's National Library. During the 1990s war between Bosnia, Serbia, and Croatia, the ancient city of Sarajevo was surrounded and besieged by the Serb army for three years. In spite of daily mortars and sniper fire, Vedran would put on his tux, take a folding chair, and play the cello. He made his way to the very places where bombs had fallen and people were killed, playing music there so the people of Sarajevo would not give up hope. Like Vedran, when you remember who you are, you can find dignity even among the ruins of your life.

If you have lost money or faith, when you are sick or a family member is suffering from illness or addiction, even when a child is in jeopardy, you are not alone. You are sharing in the inevitable trouble of human incarnation. On this very day, hundreds of thousands of others are also dealing with loss of money or a new diagnosis, or holding their sick child, sometimes alone, sometimes reaching out to others for support. Breathe with them and hold their pain with yours, sharing courage and compassion.

Two women in nearby towns in northern Canada were forced to venture out in a fierce winter storm. One was taking her pregnant daughter to the hospital; the other was driving to take care of her ill father. They made their way along the same road from opposite directions, through hurricane winds and pelting snow. Suddenly each was stopped on opposite sides of a huge fallen tree that blocked the road. It took them only a few minutes to share their stories, exchange car keys, and set forth in each other's cars to complete their journeys.

As you open beyond the self, you realize that others are part of your extended family. Sylvia Boorstein, a colleague and wisdom holder, tells how in Jewish synagogues there is a yearly memorial service for the survivors of relatives whose death dates are unknown—men and women who died in the Holocaust or are buried in unknown graves. Many people will stand for the Mourner's Kaddish prayer. In temple on this day, Sylvia writes, "I looked at the people standing and thought, 'Can all these people be direct survivors?' Then I realized we all are, and I stood up, too."

Beyond the self is not *me* connected to the *outside world*. It's *us*, interbeing. In this place, even compassion is beside the point.

Everyone Gains

Gandhi said, "When one person gains, the whole world gains. And if one person falls, the whole world falls to that extent." When you quiet your mind and open your heart, who you are is obvious. You are interdependent with all; you are life knowing itself through your body and senses, flowering, arising and re-arising. You are unstoppable. Sages and wise women, shamans and saints live within this knowing. Even when they doubt their own worthiness, they turn toward this mystery.

I've always loved the account of Black Elk, the beloved Sioux medicine man whose moving story appears in John Neihardt's book *Black Elk Speaks*. The last chapter tells of Black Elk's final hike up Harney Peak. The Sioux holy man had explained to Neihardt that when death approached, a Lakota could climb this sacred mountain to see if the Great Spirit approved of his life. Rain would fall on those who had the Great Spirit's blessing.

As a young man, Black Elk had a vision that told him how to save his people and homeland from soldiers and settlers. All of his years, he had worked to fulfill this vision and restore the sacred hoop of life. Living through tragic circumstances, he felt that he had failed and that the sacred hoop was broken. On the day of his climb, Black Elk was an old man. He dressed in red long johns, moccasins, war paint, and a feathered war headdress. Slowly and laboriously he climbed to the summit, oblivious to the tourists who were staring at him. Neihardt teased him that he should have picked a day with at least one cloud in the sky, but

Black Elk rebuked him, saying that the rain would have nothing to do with the weather.

At the top of the peak, not far from the tourists, the old man lay down under a blue sky. To his astonishment, Neihardt watched a few small clouds form over Black Elk and a soft rain begin to fall. Black Elk wept with relief. He felt that even though he had not succeeded in fulfilling his vision, the Great Spirit was recognizing that he had done his best.

Your life is not separate from the earth, the sun, and the stars, but held by and a part of all. With this realization comes joyful freedom. Trust it. Beloved Christian mystic Thomas Merton had left his cloistered monastery to go into town. There in Louisville, Kentucky, on a street corner, his vision opened:

> *At the corner of Fourth and Walnut, in the center of the shopping district, I was suddenly overwhelmed with the realization that I loved all those people, that they were mine and I theirs, that we could not be alien to one another even though we were total strangers. It was like waking from a dream of separateness, of spurious self-isolation. . . . I have the immense joy of being a member of the human race, where the divine spark is made incarnate. There is no way of telling people that they are all walking around shining like the sun.*

At this corner in downtown Louisville, there is a formal marker, a bronze historical plaque, unique in America, with these words commemorating his mystical experience. Reminding us that all places are holy.

Outer and Inner Freedom

Here is the paradox. You are one with the mystery of life, and you have your unique incarnation. You have one foot in the timeless realm and one in individual identity. Each of these realms offers the possibility of freedom.

Outer freedom allows an individual to live as he or she chooses: to have life, liberty, the pursuit of happiness, *liberté*, *égalité*, and *fraternité*. These outer freedoms are human treasures. It is an enormous blessing to enjoy freedom of speech, religion, assembly, and travel; to choose your own way of life and be treated with dignity. It is a fundamental human right to be free from oppression, injustice, or slavery; to be free from crushing poverty, economic oppression, or fear of hunger.

You may enjoy all of these freedoms, but hundreds of millions of families around the world do not. They may be politically oppressed, or ethnically persecuted, or perennially sick or hungry. The taste of freedom starts where they are. Gandhi declared, "For the hungry, freedom arrives in the form of bread." For many, a breathtaking freedom would be food or simply modest opportunity, basic human rights, or the end of war, conflict, and racism.

The great blessing is that you can use your freedom to bring freedom and benefit to others! You can unite your freedom with theirs. As your own sense of personal freedom grows, you can contribute to the well-being of the whole, taking to heart Dr. Martin Luther King's vision, "We are not free until all are free." Each person who awakens to freedom and interconnection can make an enormous difference.

In my own life, I am privileged to enjoy almost all the world's outer freedoms. In spite of a painful upbringing with a violent and abusive father, I grew up with great abundance, middle class in a wealthy nation with opportunity, health, and education. While this allowed me to seek inner freedom in the monastery, it also increased my concern for others. The struggle for outer freedom and seeking inner freedom seem to come together naturally. I have worked for the reform of prisons, peace in Burma, social justice, environmental causes, and freedom in Palestine, Tibet, and elsewhere. It has been an honor.

On a recent visit to Washington, DC, I stood at the temple of the Lincoln Memorial and gazed at the words of sacrifice and vision inscribed in marble, exhorting us ". . . with malice toward none and charity for all . . . to do all which may achieve and cherish a just and lasting peace among ourselves and with all nations." Tears filled my eyes for the weight and sacrifice that President Lincoln bore witness to and the unshakable moral leadership he showed that is so needed in today's world.

My friend Maha Ghosananda, the Gandhi of Cambodia, showed how this is still possible. The genocide of the Khmer Rouge had burned temples, killed millions, including many of those who were educated, among them all nineteen members of Maha Ghosananda's family. One of the few surviving senior monks, Ghosananda built temples for the hundreds of thousands of refugees living in border camps. When the war slowed down and it became possible to return to their homes, he told the surviving villagers that they could not simply ride buses or trucks back home. There had been too much tragedy. They needed to walk back with him, continually chanting prayers of lovingkindness, to deliberately, step by step, reclaim their land, their hearts, their country. He personally led peace walks through war zones and jungle paths, guiding refugees back to their villages.

He led group after group, year after year. While they walked— in long lines, ringing bells and singing of compassion—frightened widows would come out of hiding places in the bushes and battle-worn soldiers from both sides would lay their guns at Ghosananda's feet and weep.

Nominated for the Nobel Prize, founder of thirty temples, scholar of fifteen languages, and respected elder of the peace process at the UN, he mostly lived in the jungles and spent his years guiding others, walking, teaching, chanting the simple truth "Hatred never ceases by hatred, but by love alone is healed." He showed everyone he met that the force of love could overcome the power of hate. Maha Ghosananda demonstrated that the human heart can be free no matter where you are. Yes, you are vulnerable. Yet no matter what your struggle, you can walk with a compassionate, caring, soaring spirit.

Emptiness Is Our Home

In the same spirit, Vaclav Havel went from being locked in a Communist prison to becoming the president of Czechoslovakia, and

Burmese Nobel laureate Aung San Suu Kyi's forbearance while under house arrest for seventeen years inspired people worldwide. Even in times of terrible conflict or financial strain, illness, or divorce, you can choose your spirit.

Remember, when you feel afraid, lost, or confused, a deeper part of you never loses contact with the baseline of freedom. Let fresh air brush your skin, enter your lungs, and expand your ideas of time and space. Experiences are like waves on the ocean, moments of your seemingly individual life that crest and vanish. Despite the arising and falling of wave after wave, the ocean neither gains nor loses. What is real can never be lost.

When her first daughter was born, twenty-two-year-old Alicia had been practicing kundalini yoga for several years. She would chant, meditate, and do intense breath practices in various postures. When her contractions started, she was taken to the hospital by a friend. In the birthing room without a partner present, the contractions became powerful and at times exquisitely painful. In the first hours, Alicia was scared. Then she was taken over by the force of birthing. Her breath became rapid like kundalini breathing, her body filled with light. Her sense of Alicia dissolved. She became all mothers, human mothers, animal mothers, the earth, the stream of life giving birth to itself. She was amazed.

Alicia had read about oneness and samadhi in her yoga books. But the immensity of this experience left her tender, shaking, transformed, grateful. Grateful for the beautiful eight-pound boy at her breast. When the shaking and rapid breathing continued—along with inner lights—after the birth, the doctors prescribed Valium to "quiet her down." But she knew it wasn't a medical problem. The wind had blown open a door to the cosmos beyond herself, and she would spend her life exploring and embodying this realization.

You are not the body that changes form so many times in your lifetime. Nor are you your thoughts or personality. You are the vast ocean, the awareness, the One Who Knows. Sharon Salzberg describes seeing a homeless man beseech each passerby, "Don't you know me?" Somehow you do know him, his plea resonating poignantly in the depths of our shared being.

To the extent that you identify with your body, your feelings, your thoughts or intentions, your roles, with a limited self of time, you will be anxious and your life contracted. Vastness, the ground from which all appears, is your home. Here you are, born out of emptiness. Thoughts and experiences, days and years appear out of emptiness and then vanish. Relax and simply open. Let the mind quiet and the heart be easy. Sights and sounds and people still come and go, but all around, as vast as the galaxy, is a deep perfection and a profound silence. In the quiet mind, everything has its place—the ocean of tears and the unbearable beauty. In Zen, this is called the interplay of form and emptiness. You are the wave, seemingly separate from the deep ocean, and you are the ocean—deep, sparkling, home to billions of beings, salty like tears and vast.

Vision

Sometimes this understanding comes through a vision, as it did for Ramakrishna, the Hindu sage whose love and devotion were legendary throughout nineteenth-century India. Ramakrishna used to sit by the side of the Ganges River lost in prayer for days, seeking a revelation of the face of the Divine Mother, the Goddess creator of life itself. One day, she showed herself. The surface of the water rippled and out of the river arose an enormous and beautiful goddess with dark, shining hair cascading with the waters of the river, her eyes like pools that contain all things. Staring into Ramakrishna's eyes, she opened her legs and from her vagina a vast stream of beings were appearing, born out of her body, children and animals. She became a fountain of birth of all life. After a time, to his shock, she reached down and lifted a newborn child to her mouth and began to eat it, blood dripping down her mouth and across her breasts. She Who Creates is also known as She Who Destroys. She is the divine feminine, the source, continuation, and the ending of all life. Still looking into Ramakrishna's eyes, the goddess slowly sank down beneath the waves, leaving him to contemplate the mysterious reality beyond birth and death.

Shamans and mystics know this eternal dance. Your bodily incarnation is born of spirit, it is a play of consciousness. On a retreat that I led in New Mexico, one man had intense shoulder pain and feelings of anxiety that opened him to deep layers of memories. First, he remembered the trauma of a minor car accident the previous year, then came a deeper memory of a dislocated shoulder injury from construction work in high school. Then he remembered falling into a stream at five and being violently yanked out by the shoulder. Then, because he was a breech birth, he reexperienced his shoulder stuck in the birth canal. And finally came a vivid image from a past life where he was a foot soldier in a medieval war. His shoulder was struck by a spear and he died in the mud. He realized that his consciousness was the timeless witness of it all.

When the sage Nisargadatta was in his eighties, his disciples asked if he had any concerns about death. "Do you think I am this meat body, made of all the food I have eaten? Do you think I am the fading memories it carries?" He laughed. "You insult me. Who I am was never born and will never die. You take your body and limited life to be who you are, and so you suffer. Step out of this illusion, and you will see that you are nothing and everything. You will be free."

"I Told You So"

My father was a biophysicist who worked in space medicine, taught in medical schools, and designed some of the first artificial hearts and lungs. Though he could design a machine for the heart, expressing his heart in life was much more difficult. I learned early that there is a big difference between intelligence and human happiness.

In the last week of his life, I sat beside him at the University of Pennsylvania Medical Center in the cardiac care unit. He couldn't breathe easily; he felt a constant air hunger, even when the oxygen was fully turned on. He had congestive heart failure now at age seventy-five, after several hospitalizations and a major heart attack ten years earlier. He had been a difficult father, a paranoid, workaholic scientist with a hair-trigger temper, abusive to his family and judgmental to everyone else. It had taken years for me to work this out, and I finally felt at peace with him. So, I just sat, listening to him breathe.

Periodically he would talk about his life or mine, often with a self-serving analysis and rewriting of history. I had felt his fear in his phone calls, and it was even stronger as I sat with him. He was afraid of dying. He hadn't slept for days and was almost delusional. As a biophysicist and medical professor, he understood all the cardiac monitoring equipment now hooked up to his heart. Each time he began to fall asleep, he startled awake after a couple of minutes and quickly wrested his body around to check the monitors. Was his heart still beating? His fear was that he would die and none of the nurses would notice until it was too late.

It was hard to watch him so helpless and afraid. I practiced lovingkindness meditation as I sat, holding my father, myself, and the world in compassion with each breath. I decided to teach him a meditation, hoping to ease his anxiety. I instructed him to relax, to follow each breath gently, but he couldn't do it, not even a little. It made him even more anxious. So, I tried a simple lovingkindness practice. I asked him to picture each of his grandchildren and, using a phrase of affection, to wish each of them well, to offer them a prayer. He couldn't do that either; he was too worried and distracted. After seven decades of practicing paranoia, it was a bit late to learn to meditate. So, we just talked.

I asked him what he believed happens when you die. "Nothing," he said. "When your body dies, you go to nothingness and your ashes go to the earth, that's all." He was a scientist, a materialist, and pretty much an atheist as well. So, I told him about my out-of-body experiences and past-life memories and sitting with the dying. I reminded him that most cultures on earth, including the shamans and saints, sages and wise women all understand that there is life after death. For millennia those who have explored the inner world found that you are not just a body but also spirit. When your body dies, your spirit is released, set free. "Since you are a scientist," I suggested, "why not look at dying as an experiment." I went on cheerfully, "It could well happen that when you die, as your senses shut down, you'll feel yourself floating out of your body, entering a realm of light." He shook his head dubiously. "Well," I went on, "if it does, just remember, 'I told you so!'" He laughed.

Near midnight, after the other patients' visitors had left, I told him I needed to go to sleep and would be back in the morning. "Wait," he said. "Don't go." So, I sat with him a while longer. Exhausted, he started to drift off to sleep. Two minutes later he startled awake, fearfully wrenching around to check his life signs on the screen. Then he looked at me. "I can't sleep. Please stay." I was happy to comply. I've learned to sit. He went on, dozing and waking for hours. Each time he awoke, he pleaded for time. "Please don't go yet." For the first time since I was a little boy, he let me hold his hand. He was frightened. He didn't want to know about meditation. He didn't want to contemplate his imminent passing. He didn't even want to talk. What mattered was just sitting with him there, not being afraid, and touching him.

Perhaps that's all we can do for others, to hold them with kindness and our deepest presence. The gift we can offer is the faith and confidence we have in life. Freedom of spirit is what I offered my father. Born from loving awareness, mysterious, magnificent, and simple, it is always here, available.

PRACTICE
Open to Mystery

You can step into mystery wherever you are, with an open, curious wonder. Here you are, on this astonishing planet, in this spiral galaxy, with language and love and an invitation to see.

- Lie outside on the grass on a warm starlit night. Imagine that you are at the bottom of the turning world (there really is no top or bottom), held on by the magnet of gravity. Look up into the infinite sea of stars.

- Hold your breath for a minute or more. Feel how your body finally insists on breathing. It is ever breathing, living with the air that dusts mountaintops and passes across oceans, through the lungs of deer, the leaves of oaks and maples, automobile engines, and the South Pole. Feel how you are part of the earth breathing.

- Ask yourself: How did you get here in this human life? What is mind? What is love? What will happen next month? When will you die? What is death? Where do stars come from?? What will the human world look like in twenty-five years?

Pause after each question and let the feeling of "don't know" open you to mystery. Relax and enjoy the mystery, rest in the vast mystery that holds and supports you and all life. You are the mystery seeing itself.

• Contemplate the mystery of your body. The trillion patterns of synaptic connections in your brain, the 100 trillion bacteria in your gut. Your liver is processing a million complex reactions right now, your body is awash in fluids and tubes of blood and lymph and bile and urine and spinal fluid, all flowing like the infrastructure of Manhattan. And all collaborating in a mysterious dance to protect your life.

• Look into the eyes of a young child. See the child of the spirit, the mystery born into this new form. Where did they come from? What will they become?

• Get a teaspoon of soil. It has a billion bacteria, millions of fungi, hundreds of thousands of microarthropods, thousands of protozoa and nematodes. More life in one spoonful than on all of the other planets combined.

• Go to a cemetery. Contemplate death.

• Go to a dating website. Contemplate desire and love.

PRACTICE
Just Like Me

This is a practice to be done in pairs. It can be done in a group, with one person reading these words aloud, or go to jackkornfield.com for a free download where I read this to you.

Sit across from another person; it may be someone you know well or a person in your office or school.

Let yourself gaze appreciatively at the other person. When you can, look into their eyes. If you experience any nervousness or laughter or feel shy, just note this embarrassment with patience and kindness and return when you can to your partner's gaze. It is remarkable to truly see one another in this mystery.

Looking deeply, see the consciousness behind those eyes. Contemplate each phrase as you hear it:

This person is incarnated in a body, going through life just like me.

This person was once a small child, a little, vulnerable child, just like me.

This person has had happy times in their life, just like me.

This person is creative, just like me.

This person has loved someone, just like me.

This person's heart has been broken, just like me.

This person has had their measure of sorrow and sadness, just like me.

This person has been hurt and disappointed, just like me.

This person has been confused by life, just like me.

This person has helped others, just like me.

This person will be young and old, friend and enemy, just like me.

This person has known physical pain, just like me.

This person has regrets, just like me.

This person wants to be loved, just like me.

This person wants to be safe and healthy, just like me.

Look deeply. Behind these eyes is the original spirit, born into each one of us.

Picture this person's happiest moments as a child; laughing, playing, joyful times.

I know this child of the spirit is still in you, just like me.

I wish you to be happy and your joy to increase, because I know you want to be happy, just like me.

I wish you strength and support in your life so that you can do what is best for you and offer your gifts to yourself and the world, just like me.

I wish for you blessings and courage, love and compassion, for you are a precious human being, just like me.

Chapter 15

The Joy of Being Alive

*Now and then it's good to pause in your pursuit
of happiness, and just be happy.*

—GUILLAUME APOLLINAIRE

After Yolanda's son Pete was killed, she would wake up each night and weep, caught in a prison of grief and regret. On the first anniversary of his death, she lit a memorial candle before going to bed. Just as she was falling asleep, Pete came to her in a vision. He was shining like a bright spirit. "Mom," he said, "I don't want to see you like this, living with such a heavy heart. I love you so much, but it was my time. This is something you can't do anything about. Please, Mom, live again. And I'll be with you."

Yolanda shed tears of release and relief, and her weary heart softened. She stayed up quietly for hours, thinking of Pete and her own life and the good years they'd had, letting his luminous message touch her again and again. In the morning, she woke up renewed. Life was precious again. "I decided to begin fresh. I now carry Pete's spirit with me. I work and garden and travel and care for family and others with a joyful heart. People now want to be around me, seeing you can always start again."

Happiness for No Cause

Japan's beloved Zen poet Ryokan was known for being unpretentious and wise. Like Saint Francis, he was a lover of simple things, of children and nature. In his poems, he wrote openly of his tears and loneliness during long winter nights, of his heart leaping with spring blossoms, of his losses and regrets and the deep trust he learned. His emotions flowed freely, like the seasons. When people asked about enlightenment, he offered them tea. When he went to the village for alms and to offer teachings, he often ended up playing with the children. His happiness came from a profound peace with himself.

Today's begging is finished: at the crossroads
I wander by the side of the Buddhist shrine
Talking with some children.
Last year, a foolish monk.
This year, no change!

We are human, no more, no less. When we accept our humanness, a remarkable transformation can take place. Tenderness and wisdom arise naturally. Where we once sought strength over others, our true strength is now our own. Where we once sought to defend ourselves, now we can laugh. Allowing room for our vulnerability and needs brings forth a hidden courage. Happiness and love come naturally when we let go of posturing, of trying to be who we are not, who we think we should be. Joy bubbles up like spring water and spreads throughout our being.

Bouncing for Joy

As a world icon, the Dalai Lama has tens of thousands of people attend his talks. Yes, they go for the profound Tibetan teachings and to support his nonviolent, compassionate efforts to overcome his country's loss of freedom and culture. But I think, most of all they go to hear him laugh. They want to see his quick smile and hear his charming giggle that brings tears to his and others' eyes.

When the Dalai Lama offered the solemn Kalachakra teachings at Madison Square Garden, his hosts had put a mattress on his "throne" under brocade and a beautiful Tibetan rug, so he would be comfortable. As he walked up the stairs onto the platform and sat down on the throne amid great gongs and deep, resonant Tibetan chanting, he bounced. Surprised, he smiled and bounced again, and again. There he was, about to give the highest Tibetan teachings on the creation of the cosmos and the release from time, on a throne in front of thousands of people, and he sat there bouncing like a kid. How can a man who has witnessed so much suffering be that joyful? "They have taken the sacred texts from our temples, put our monks in prison, taken so much from the Tibetan people," he says. "Why should I also let them take my happiness?"

Buddhist psychology encourages us to develop the best capacities of human well-being. It describes dozens of kinds of joy and happiness, including smiling joy, cool thrilling joy, floating joy, light-filled joy, trembling energetic joy, joy in the beauty of the world, deep silent happiness, bodily happiness, happiness of mental well-being, and unshakable happiness of the heart. The Buddha instructed his students to find joy everywhere:

> *Live in joy, in love,*
> *even among those who hate.*
> *Live in joy, in health,*
> *even among the afflicted.*
> *Live in joy, in peace,*
> *even among the troubled.*
> *Free from fear and attachment,*
> *Know the sweet joy of the Way.*

Even in this difficult world, don't hesitate to laugh and love and enjoy yourself and others! Within you was born *joie de vivre*, the great heart of life that wants to celebrate. Trust in this.

Gratefulness

When I was eight years old, I was diagnosed with polio and taken to the hospital at St. Louis University Medical School, where my father was teaching. I had a high fever and was partially paralyzed. The old wooden hospital building was creaky and dark at night, and it was scary being there, feverish, unable to move. I remember the pain of the spinal taps done with a huge horse needle and no anesthesia. Outside my window, I could see a small lawn and longed to escape.

Unexpectedly, after some weeks the symptoms disappeared. I was so grateful. I remember being driven home. As soon as I could I walked to the little park down the block from where I lived, and I rolled on the grass like a dog, then began dancing and jumping, I was so happy just to be able to walk, to be able to move. I was filled with gratitude. I felt the joy of life, being happy just where I was.

We all face hardship, but how do we move through it? Every new stage of life asks this question. When my long marriage ended, I was brokenhearted and discouraged. I left a beautiful home and moved into my one-room writer's cabin and emotionally felt my life approaching age sixty-five was nearly over. Having to write a new will brought the end of life further into stark view. Though I was still teaching and writing, I didn't know what else to do with myself.

I meditated, and made space, and waited. After a lonely time,

I considered dating, but the idea of dating seemed strange and horrible. I went anyway and tried a few awkward dates. All along I had been teaching with my colleagues, and one of my favorites was Trudy Goodman. We had an easy and playful collaboration when we worked together. Her spiritual depth and joyful heart were like medicine, just what I needed. We talked more, and our connection became more loving and fun.

I slowly remembered that it's never too late to start over. So, we began tentatively to be together.

Slowly I became ready to let go and start anew. This started a whole new life for me. We began to travel and teach and fell in love. Because Trudy has one of the most joyful spirits of anyone I know, I was caught by her joy. She laughs easily, is game for wild adventure, and is enthusiastic about almost everything. We laugh about how wonderful it is to be together, recently married, now in our seventies, so grateful for the time we have. I returned to joy. And you can, too.

Debra Chamberlin-Taylor, a friend and colleague, shares the story of a community activist who participated in her yearlong training for women of color. In her childhood, this woman had experienced poverty, trauma, and abuse. She had faced the loss of a parent, illness, an early divorce from a painful marriage, and racism while bringing up two children on her own. She spoke to the group about her struggles to educate herself and stand up for what she believed, how in the years since graduating from UC Berkeley, she had become a radical voice for the abused and the unrepresented in local and national politics. At the group's last meeting, she announced, "After all the struggles and troubles I've lived through, I've decided to do something *really* radical. I am going to be happy!"

Pure Heart

Jasper was labeled a child with Down syndrome. In his case, his parents explained, it should have been called "Up syndrome." Every morning when he woke up, he rushed into his parents' bedroom and leaped on them with an enthusiastic "Happy to you morning!" He meets the entire world with his heart outstretched and hugs everyone he can. They used to call his state "retarded." Parents of similar children warned Jasper's parents to curb his hugging behavior or he could be the target of molesters. They disagreed, knowing Jasper's loving nature was his gift.

One day, Jasper and his parents were walking down the street and Jasper got out in front of them. He was almost twelve by then, but still very small. An angry-looking man with tattoos and piercings came toward him, and Jasper's mom thought, Uh-oh. But it was too late. Jasper looked up, smiled, and threw his arms around the man's legs, shouting, "Hi, there!" The tough guy paused and tousled Jasper's hair, and then his mom saw this innocent-looking smile come over his tough-guy face. Jasper had done his magic again.

You can relearn happiness and come back in touch with your own pure heart. Even if you are in the middle of difficulties—an emergency at work, a relative in the hospital, or a pressing obligation—take a moment to breathe and pause, and touch your heart.

Create the space for your kindest, most natural response, rather than the fear and tension that often control the mind.

Neuroscience explains why this requires practice. Your brain is wired with a negative bias—evolution has trained you to first scan for dangers, to pick up any potential threats, and to protect yourself. Fortunately, happiness is also innate. But to truly embody it, you need to train yourself to turn toward moments of well-being and joy, to invite, foster, and then learn to dwell in them. As the poet Rumi explains, "When you go to a garden, do you look at thorns or flowers? Spend more time with roses and jasmine." There is a beautiful practice for the cultivation of joy. Like the practices of love and compassion, the cultivation of joy uses simple heartfelt phrases of your best intention. Begin by bringing to mind someone you care about, someone it's easy to rejoice for. Imagine their happiest day as a young child, their innate and beautiful spirit. Feel the natural joy you have for their well-being, for their happiness and success. With each breath, offer them your grateful, heartfelt wishes:

May you be joyful.
May your joy increase.
May you not be separated from great happiness.
May your good fortune and the causes of your joy and happiness increase.

Sense the sympathetic joy and caring in each phrase. When you feel some degree of joy for this loved one, extend this practice to another person you care about. Recite the same simple phrases that express your heart's intention.

Then gradually open the meditation to other loved ones and benefactors. After the joy for them grows strong, turn back to include yourself. Let the feelings of joy begin to fill your body and mind. Continue repeating the intentions of joy over and over, through whatever resistances and difficulties arise, until you feel stabilized in joy. Next you can include other friends, loved ones, neutral people, then difficult people, and even enemies until you extend sympathetic joy to all beings everywhere, young and old, near and far.

Practice dwelling in joy until the deliberate effort of practice drops away and the intentions of joy blend into the natural joy of your own wise heart.

You Deserve Happiness

Perhaps you're afraid of happiness, feeling that somehow you don't deserve it. You have become loyal to your suffering. Yes, you need to treat your suffering and the suffering of the world honorably. If a sick child has kept you up all night, or you've been in an accident, or you're struggling with someone difficult, hold the suffering tenderly—respond with compassionate action, grieve, heal what is possible. But suffering is not the end of the story.

I've watched orphaned children in desolate refugee camps joyfully racing cars made out of sticks and evaporated-milk cans, their spirits untrammeled. I've seen Maha Ghosananda, who lost so much in the tragedy of Cambodia's killing fields, smile from love, never letting tragedy overcome his spirit. André Gide, who won the Nobel Prize for literature, wrote, "Know that joy is rarer, more difficult and more beautiful than sadness. Once you make this all-important discovery, you must embrace joy as a moral obligation."

What about the suffering of the world? How *dare* we be joyful in the face of so much sorrow? In "A Brief for the Defense," poet Jack Gilbert responds:

Sorrow everywhere. Slaughter everywhere. If babies
are not starving someplace, they are starving
somewhere else. With flies in their nostrils.
But we enjoy our lives because that's what God wants.
Otherwise the mornings before summer dawn would not
be made so fine. The Bengal tiger would not
be fashioned so miraculously well. The poor women
at the fountain are laughing together between
the suffering they have known and the awfulness
in their future, smiling and laughing while somebody
in the village is very sick . . .
If we deny our happiness, resist our satisfaction,
we lessen the importance of their deprivation.
We must risk delight. We can do without pleasure,
but not delight. Not enjoyment. We must have
the stubbornness to accept our gladness in the ruthless
furnace of this world. To make injustice the only

measure of our attention is to praise the Devil.
If the locomotive of the Lord runs us down,
we should give thanks that the end had magnitude.
We must admit there will be music despite everything.

When you are loyal to your suffering, wrapped up in your own pain and trauma, it can offer a familiar sense of identity, meaning, and purpose. You might not know yourself without your suffering. But when you release your suffering, it can become your gateway to dignity, compassion, and a deeper freedom. You are bigger than your wounds.

Wonderful!

Though we all want to be happy, often we don't know how. Even self-destructive acts like addiction, violence, or suicide can be misguided efforts to reduce pain. Happiness invites you to look beyond your painful story. Feel the breeze as you step outdoors. Alison Luterman instructs you to notice how: "Sun drapes a buttered scarf across your face, rose opens herself to your glance, and rain shares its divine melancholy. The whole world keeps whispering or shouting to you, nibbling your ear like a neglected lover."

Sometimes, when you need help, you can catch the spirit of happiness from another. Martina was a physician and the administrator of a medical school hospital. Her work often took her to the cafeteria, where she got to know Annabelle, a Haitian woman who worked in the kitchen. Annabelle had worked there for twenty-five years and now, in her sixties, was supporting seven grandchildren. Petite and strong, Annabelle had lived through years of hardship and loss, yet each time Martina asked her how she was doing, Annabelle would turn up her face with a bright smile and say not just "okay" or "fine" or even "great," but *"Wonderful!"* It was audacious and true. You could feel it. In the drab cafeteria kitchen, endless hard work, a tough life, and "Wonderful." To Martina, Annabelle's voice became a bell of mindfulness transforming the world. Whenever she felt frustrated or sorry for herself, she would smile like Annabelle and say to herself, *"Wonderful!"*

Happiness is your birthright. You are born radiant, a child of the earth, innocent, open, and filled with wonder. As Emerson describes, we arrive "trailing clouds of glory." Then you find yourself embodied and vulnerable and, inevitably, you experience the full measure of life's pleasure and pain. Navigating this terrain is the challenge and blessing of human life.

The deepest happiness is also there for you, a wellspring beyond your fear. It flows from the creative river of life's mystery. This is why ninety-year-old widows tend small flowers in spring gardens and ten-year-olds with little to eat care for stray kittens. It is why painters going blind paint more, and composers going deaf write exquisite symphonies. As you give yourself to life, the river of life flows through you and renews itself.

It's in Your Hands

In the end, you can be happy no matter what. Sometimes you remember it from Annabelle's smile, sometimes through appreciating what you have. When your small sense of self feels vulnerable and traumatized and threatened by life, it lives in fear, constricted. Yes, you will be subject to the vicissitudes of life, but often a terrible experience is not as devastating as you'd imagined it would be. You can start again, here and now. Let the mind quiet and the mystery of life offer its gifts in return. This happiness is born just where you are.

A. Dioxides writes about the lessons of life he learned from an old man in an Athenian tavern:

Night after night he sat alone at the same table, drinking wine with precisely the same gestures. I finally asked him why he did this and he said, "Young man, I first look at my glass to please my eyes, then I take it in my hand to please my hand. Then I bring it to my nose to please my nostrils, and I am just about to bring it to my lips when I hear a small voice in my ears, 'How about me?' So, I tap my glass on the table before I drink from it. Then I please all the senses. And this, when I act, I act with my whole being."

As your loving attention grows, you can tend yourself and the world with more care, you promote joy and well-being. I learned from a friend, one of America's leading writers, about self-care. She was scheduled to speak at an all-day benefit for a beloved nonprofit and she'd been flattened, sick, feverish with a strong virus. She managed to go and read and teach for a bit of the day, and then she came back home. Later she explained that she had to take care of herself, no one else could do that. Even though the attendees were sympathetic, she said, they would go home and talk about how it was to see this world-famous writer teach when she was very sick. Yes, they were interested and caring. "But if I died up there, folks would go home with the story, 'Wow, I was there when she died.'"

Nobody can tend your life for you. It's in your own hands and heart. Always, you are invited and required to find your own way.

A school principal who lived in the Tenderloin district in San Francisco liked to make sandwiches for the homeless. Several hours a day after school, if she wasn't tired, she took pleasure in preparing the food. Then she'd go down and distribute it on the streets. She didn't care if she was thanked or sometimes refused. She was doing it because it was what felt right to do. After some time, the local media found out about it, and she became a minor celebrity in her area. Inspired by her work, other teachers and colleagues began to send her money for her ministry. To their surprise, they all received their money back with the short note "Make your own damn sandwiches."

Coursing in Gratitude

Ben Franklin enjoyed reflecting daily on the happiness he experienced by practicing temperance, silence, order, and other virtues he valued. Naikan, a Japanese practice of self-reflection, empha-sizes reviewing your life and coursing in gratitude. When Aung Sang Suu Kyi was released after seventeen years of house arrest, I felt a sympathetic happiness for her as when I was released from the hospital in St. Louis. When she walked out of her house a free person, her dignity, grace, and beauty were palpable. She showed incredible graciousness, good heart, and clarity of mind. Suu Kyi seemed joyful and remarkably present, as though she'd just come out of a long retreat, which of course she had.

Imagine getting a phone call from your doctor: "Your tests don't look so good, you need to come in, we need to talk about this." Your mind races; you have a bad diagnosis. But later it turns out to be wrong and you are okay. And you go, "Oh my God, thank you, I have my life back, it's wonderful to be alive." That is gratitude. That is happiness. That is mindful awareness, loving awareness—to be able to walk, to breathe, to be alive, grateful for the whole beautiful, unruly dance of your life. Gratitude is not dependent on what you have. It depends on your heart. You can even find gratitude for your measure of sorrows, the hand you've been dealt. There is mystery surrounding even your difficulties and suffering. Sometimes it's through the hardest things that your heart learns its most important lessons.

Freedom and joy are not grim duties or a withdrawal from life. They are the innate wonder of spirit, the blessings of gratitude, the prayers of appreciation, the aliveness of being. They are the free heart rejoicing in the morning sunlight, the sturdy grasses and breath carried by the winds over the mountains. The world is a temple, a sanctuary, bathed even at night by the miraculous light of the ocean of stars that never stop shining upon us. Every meeting of eyes, every leafing oak, every taste of raspberry and warm-baked loaf is a blessing. These are the sacred notes in the symphony of life, the invitation to discover freedom, the joyful magnificence of a free and loving heart. They are yours and everyone's to share.

Acknowledgments
and Bows of Gratitude

To Trudy Goodman, wife, partner, colleague, and beloved, who has made my life so joyful and full of love.

To Arnie Kotler, friend and magician of an editor, who took this manuscript and made it sing.

To Leslie Meredith, master editor and supporter, who has patiently and faithfully stewarded my books and work.

To Sara Sparling, my caring, delightful, and faithful assistant, who helped with much of these pages.

To special men, Wes Nisker, Phillip Moffitt, Stan Grof, and Michael Meade.

To my amazing circle of colleagues from whom I have learned so much.

To my teachers, Ajahn Chah, Mahasi Sayadaw, Sri Nisargadatta, Ajahn Buddhadasa, Ram Dass, Kalu Rinpoche, Seung Sahn, Hameed Ali, and many others.

To Caroline, who serves so beautifully, the wisest and coolest daughter.

To my brothers all.

Index

Credits

About the Author

Jack Kornfield trained as a Buddhist monk in the monasteries of Thailand, India, and Burma. He has taught meditation internationally since 1974 and is one of the key teachers to introduce Buddhist mindfulness practice to the West. After graduating from Dartmouth College in Asian Studies in 1967, he joined the Peace Corps and worked on tropical medicine teams in the Mekong River valley. He met and studied as a monk under the Buddhist master Ven. Ajahn Chah, as well as the Ven. Mahasi Sayadaw of Burma. Returning to the United States, Jack cofounded the Insight Meditation Society in Barre, Massachusetts, together with Sharon Salzberg and Joseph Goldstein, and then the Spirit Rock Center in Woodacre, California. Over the years, Jack has taught in centers and universities worldwide, led International Buddhist Teacher meetings, and worked with many of the great spiritual teachers of our time. He holds a PhD in clinical psychology and is a father, husband, and activist.

His books have been translated into twenty languages and sold more than a million copies. They include *The Wise Heart*; *A*

Path with Heart; After the Ecstasy, the Laundry; Teachings of the Buddha; Seeking the Heart of Wisdom; Living Dharma; A Still Forest Pool; Soul Food; Buddha's Little Instruction Book; The Art of Forgiveness, Lovingkindness, and Peace; and his most recent book, *Bringing Home the Dharma: Awakening Right Where You Are.*